GENDER AND LEADERSHIP

SAGE SWIFTS

In 1976 SAGE published a series of short 'university papers', which led to the publication of the QASS series (or the 'little green books' as they became known to researchers). More than 40 years since the release of the first 'little green book', SAGE is delighted to offer a new series of swift, short and topical pieces in the ever-growing digital environment.

SAGE *Swifts* offer authors a new channel for academic research with the freedom to deliver work outside the conventional length of journal articles. The series aims to give authors speedy access to academic audiences through digital-first publication, space to explore ideas thoroughly, yet at a length which can be readily digested, and the quality stamp and reassurance of peer review.

GENDER AND LEADERSHIP

GARY N. POWELL

SAGE SWIFTS

Los Angeles | London | New Delhi
Singapore | Washington DC

Los Angeles | London | New Delhi
Singapore | Washington DC | Melbourne

SAGE Publications Ltd
1 Oliver's Yard
55 City Road
London EC1Y 1SP

SAGE Publications Inc.
2455 Teller Road
Thousand Oaks, California 91320

SAGE Publications India Pvt Ltd
B 1/I 1 Mohan Cooperative Industrial Area
Mathura Road
New Delhi 110 044

SAGE Publications Asia-Pacific Pte Ltd
3 Church Street
#10-04 Samsung Hub
Singapore 049483

Editor: Ruth Stitt
Assistant editor: Jessica Moran
Production editor: Manmeet Kaur Tura
Copyeditor: Peter Williams
Proofreader: Clare Weaver
Indexer: David Rudeforth
Marketing manager: Abigail Sparks
Cover design: Sheila Tong
Typeset by: Cenveo Publisher Services

Library of Congress Control Number: 2020938150

British Library Cataloguing in Publication data

A catalogue record for this book is available from the British Library

ISBN 978-1-5297-0911-7
eISBN 978-1-5297-3625-0

To KJN Mike Bogdanski and SBN Kristin Duethorn

who show that true leadership has no gender

CONTENTS

About the Author   viii

Acknowledgments   x

1. Why Are We Talking about the Linkage between Gender
and Leadership?   1

2. Why Do Leader Stereotypes Emphasize Masculinity?   9

3. Why Are There So Few Women in Top Management Positions?   21

4. Is There a Female Advantage or Disadvantage in the Managerial
Ranks?   39

5. Why Do (Some) Men in Top Management Feel Free to Sexually
Harass Women?   57

6. What Actions Would Work Toward Undoing the Linkage between
Gender and Leadership?   76

References   86

Index   106

ABOUT THE AUTHOR

Gary N. Powell is Professor Emeritus of Management at the University of Connecticut in Storrs, CT. He is author of *Women and Men in Management* (5th ed.), *Making Work and Family Work: From Hard Choices to Smart Choices*, and *Managing a Diverse Workforce: Learning Activities* (3rd ed.), and the editor of *Handbook of Gender and Work*. He is an internationally recognized scholar and educator on gender and diversity in the workplace and on the work–family interface. His graduate course on Women and Men in Management won an award on innovation in education from the Committee on Equal Opportunity for Women of the American Assembly of Collegiate Schools of Business (AACSB). He has received the University of Connecticut President's Award for Promoting Multiculturalism.

He has served as Chair of the Women in Management (now Gender and Diversity in Organizations) Division of the Academy of Management and received both the Janet Chusmir Service Award for his contributions to the division and the Sage Scholarship Award for his contributions to research on gender in organizations. He has received the Richard Whipp Lifetime Achievement Award of the British Academy of Management for his contributions to business and management research in the UK. He has received the Ellen Galinsky Generative Researcher Award of the Work and Family Researchers Network and was also named as a Top Ten Extraordinary Contributor for his contributions to work and family research. He has served as Distinguished Scholar at Lancaster University Management School in Lancaster, UK. He has published over 120 articles in journals such as *Academy of Management Journal, Academy of Management Review, Journal of Applied Psychology, Journal of Management, Personnel Psychology, Organizational Behavior and Human Decision Processes, Journal of Business Venturing, Journal of Vocational Behavior, Journal of Organizational Behavior, Journal of Occupational and Organizational Psychology, Entrepreneurship Theory and Practice*, and *Human Relations*, contributed over 30 chapters to edited volumes, and made over 170 presentations at professional conferences. He is a Fellow of the British Academy of Management, Academy of Social Sciences, and Eastern Academy of Management. He has served on the Board of Governors of the Academy of Management and as President of the Eastern Academy of Management. He has served as Co-editor of a Special Issue of the *Academy of Management Review* on work–life theory and on the Editorial Board of the *Academy of Management Review*, *Journal of Management*, *Journal of Management Studies*, *Human Relations*, and *Academy of Management Executive*.

Prior to joining the faculty at UConn, he worked at General Electric, graduating from its Manufacturing Management Program. At GE, he designed and implemented automated project scheduling systems as well as systems for inventory control, materials procurement, and so on. He has provided management training and development for many companies, including Webster Financial Corp., the Hartford Financial Services Group, the Implementation Partners (TIP), GE-Capital, General Signal, Apple Computer, Monroe Auto Equipment, AllState, and CIGNA, and has conducted numerous other workshops.

He holds a doctorate in organizational behavior and a master's degree in management science from the University of Massachusetts, and a bachelor's degree in management from MIT.

ACKNOWLEDGMENTS

Many people contributed to the preparation of this book. I wish to express my deepest gratitude to:

Tony Butterfield, with whom most of my personal research on gender and leadership has been conducted, for being my life-long mentor, collaborator, colleague, and friend and for all the fun we have had along the way.

My many colleagues in professional associations – the Gender and Diversity in Organizations Division (formerly Women in Management Division) and the Careers Division of the Academy of Management, the Gender in Management Special Interest Group of the British Academy of Management, and the Work and Family Researchers Network – for providing both a forum for the sharing of research findings and a stimulus for creative thinking on this topic.

The School of Business at the University of Connecticut, for its ongoing support over the course of my academic career.

Ruth Stitt at Sage Publications, for being an engaged, encouraging, and supportive editor.

Mosey the Cat, for unlimited love, affection, and play.

Laura Graves, for standing by me all the way.

WHY ARE WE TALKING ABOUT THE LINKAGE BETWEEN GENDER AND LEADERSHIP?

This book represents an extended essay on the state of knowledge regarding the linkage between gender and leadership. It is intended to provide a personal perspective on as well as an overview of issues regarding gender and leadership. It is also intended to provide a useful resource to both scholars who are subject specialists, and scholars and students who have an interest in this topic. It draws upon research on gender and leadership conducted worldwide in several disciplines, including management and organizational behavior, human resource management, psychology, sociology, economics, communications, and gender studies.

The linkage between gender and leadership, which historically has favored men and disadvantaged women, is troubling and problematic from an equal opportunity and social justice perspective. It has been a major topic of interest in the broader literature on gender issues in the workplace that has significantly grown since the 1970s (e.g., Acker, 1990; Alvesson & Due Billing, 2009; Bartol, 1978; Broadbridge & Hearn, 2008; Broadbridge & Simpson, 2011; Calás & Smircich, 1996; Davidson & Cooper, 1992; Elliott & Stead, 2008; Kanter, 1977; Kumra et al., 2014; Marshall, 1984; Mavin et al., 2014; Ryan & Haslam, 2005; Vinnicombe et al., 2013), including edited volumes of classic articles (e.g., Gatrell et al., 2010).

Nonetheless, the book arrives at a time when some have speculated that "gender fatigue" (Joshi et al., 2015, p. 1466), or weariness with researching gender issues in the workplace, has set in among scholars. Such fatigue, if it exists, may be a response to the marginalization or de-legitimation of scholarship on gender-related issues by other scholars who find them unworthy of interest (Jané et al., 2018). Gender fatigue may also arise from what has been called a "postfeminist sensibility" at work (Gill et al., 2017, p. 226). According to this sensibility, gender inequalities existed in the past (not in the present); gender inequalities occur elsewhere (not in my place of work); being a woman is an advantage (not a disadvantage); and, if any gender inequalities exist, that's just the way the workplace is and it needs to be accepted (Gill et al., 2017). In short, a postfeminist sensibility suggests that "the problem of gender has been 'solved'" as much as it ever needed to be solved (Broadbridge & Simpson, 2011, p. 475).

However, rest assured that you will find *no* gender fatigue in this corner. Indeed, I feel that we as scholars are, or should be, just getting warmed up in examining the linkage between gender and leadership because (1) even though it may have evolved, this linkage persists; and (2) it has serious consequences for individuals, organizations, and the conduct of work.

Further, heightened and sustained public interest in the linkage between gender and leadership begs our attention as scholars. For example, in recent years, extensive media attention has been devoted to the periodic rise and fall of the small number of female CEOs of large corporations (e.g., Zarya, 2018), the appropriate role of masculinity in leadership given the "hyper-masculine" leadership style of Donald Trump as US president (Powell et al., 2018) and the release of guidelines for counselors regarding the mental health hazards of expecting males to be highly masculine (American Psychological Association, 2018), and rampant sexual harassment by male top executives directed towards women seeking employment or advancement (e.g., Kantor & Twohey, 2017) and the emergence of a #MeToo Movement in response (e.g., Peters & Besley, 2019); new examples are regularly arising. Popular interest in this topic remains strong and shows no signs of going away. As the book describes in detail, important issues regarding the linkage between gender and leadership that draw considerable public attention continue to warrant our attention as scholars.

In this chapter, I first offer my perspective on some of the issues that arise when examining gender as a construct and group differences on the basis of gender. Next, I describe how I became involved in examining the topic of gender and leadership and how my answer to the question posed in the chapter's title has evolved over four decades of researching and writing about it. Finally, I introduce specific research questions regarding the linkage between gender and leadership to be addressed in the next four chapters, with a conclusions chapter to follow.

ON EXAMINING GENDER AND GENDER DIFFERENCES

First, I wish to explain my choice of terminology on the gender side of the gender-leadership linkage. (On the leadership side of this linkage, I use the terms "leader" and "manager" interchangeably as in the leadership literature.) Some scholars distinguish between sex and gender (e.g., Archer & Lloyd, 2002; Lippa, 2005; Unger, 1979). When this distinction is made, the term "sex" is used to refer to the demographic characteristic that is associated with biological characteristics of individuals such as their physiological properties and reproductive apparatus, whereas the term "gender" is used to refer to the psychosocial implications of being female or male. These implications include gender stereotypes, defined as beliefs about the psychological traits that are characteristic of males vis-à-vis females (Ellemers, 2018); gender (or "sex-role") identity, defined as beliefs about the extent to which one possesses traits associated with gender stereotypes (Bem, 1974); gender roles, defined as beliefs about the behaviors that are appropriate for males vis-à-vis females (Wood & Eagly, 2010); gender socialization, defined as the processes by which individuals learn gender stereotypes and roles beginning in childhood (Martin & Ruble, 2009); gender schemas, defined as multifaceted, internally consistent sets of ideas that people have about gender (Bem, 1993); and so on. This distinction refers to sex as "something that 'is,'" whereas it refers to gender as "something that is 'done,' 'accomplished,' or 'performed'" (Ahl, 2006, p. 597). The distinction can be important. For example, sex as a biological variable and gender as a socially constructed variable have differential consequences for human health (Cretella et al., 2019).

However, many scholars have relied on the term "gender" to refer to the phenomena being studied, including similarities and differences in the attitudes, behaviors, skills, values, and interests exhibited by females when compared with males (often referred to as gender, not sex, similarities and differences; e.g., Hyde, 2005, 2014) and gender-related phenomena such as those described above (gender stereotypes, identities, roles, socialization, schemas, etc.). These phenomena also include the processes by which institutions such as organizations, economies, and societies become "gendered" or "do gender" (Acker, 1990; Calás & Smircich, 1996; Ridgeway, 1991; Risman, 2004; West & Zimmerman, 1987). For example, gendered organizational processes may include gendered divisions of labor, authority, and the value of work; gendered perpetration of and reactions to sexual harassment; and gendered symbols and images in advertising and publicity materials (Broadbridge & Hearn, 2008). Accordingly, rather than distinguish between sex and gender as in much of my prior research (see Powell, 2019), I use the term *gender* throughout this book to avoid possible confusion and to be consistent with prevailing terminology in the gender (not sex and gender) literature.

Now that we have settled on terminology, it is important to acknowledge that gender, when considered as a demographic characteristic, does not constitute a binary variable and may be continuous (Hyde et al., 2019; Reilly, 2019); that is, not all people may be classified as being either exclusively female or exclusively male. For example, intersex people possess physical characteristics associated with both females and males, and transgender people identify with a gender different from the one assigned at birth and may undergo a physical transition so that they become members of the gender with which they identify (Köllen, 2016). However, because most scholarship on the linkage between gender and leadership has examined the experiences of women vis-à-vis those of men when group comparisons have been made, I will focus on this distinction in the book.

Many theories have been offered and much research has been conducted on various aspects of the linkage between gender and leadership. Early scholars tended to distinguish between *person-centered theories*, which focus on the suitability of women's traits, skills, and behaviors vis-à-vis those of men for leader roles, and *situation-centered theories*, which focus on the influence of work environments experienced by women vis-à-vis men in leader roles (Riger & Galligan, 1980). More recently, the emphasis of scholarly attention has shifted to *social-system-centered theories*, which focus on gendered societal processes that influence the enactment of leadership (Calás et al., 2014). Blurring the distinction between these types of theories, social-system-centered theories may be offered for person-centered and situation-centered phenomena, and situation-centered theories may be offered for person-centered phenomena. Examples of person-centered, situation-centered, and social-system-centered theories and both confirming and disconfirming evidence will be provided throughout the book.

Intersectionality refers to the notion that multiple identities intersect or overlap to shape individuals' experiences in complex ways (Acker, 2006; Ridgeway & Kricheli-Katz, 2013; Rodriguez et al., 2016; Rosette et al., 2018). Although the book is intended to focus primarily on the linkage between gender and leadership, the intersection of gender and other personal characteristics such as race and ethnicity, sexual orientation, national origin, religion, socioeconomic class, age, and so on may also be linked to leadership. However, issues of intersectionality are frequently ignored in research.

For example, most studies of the linkage between gender and leadership have not examined the influence of the racial or ethnic group of the individuals who were the focus of the study. By ignoring issues of race and ethnicity, such studies reflect an underlying assumption that gender similarities and differences in leadership-related phenomena are essentially the same for members of different racial and ethnic groups (Smooth, 2010). When the intersection of gender and other personal characteristics such as sexual orientation (Bowleg, 2008) and national origin and religion (Arifeen & Gatrell, 2020) is factored in, the list of assumptions previously made about gender similarities and differences in leadership-related phenomena across members of different groups grows. We need to guard against making such assumptions ourselves.

Finally, it is important to address what makes gender differences in leadership-related phenomena meaningful. A massive literature has accumulated over time on similarities and differences between women and men in almost everything measurable, and reviews of this literature go back more than a century (e.g., Kumra et al., 2014; Maccoby & Jacklin, 1974; Woolley, 1910). Over time, the nature of literature reviews on gender similarities and differences has shifted from narrative reviews to meta-analyses, which synthesize statistical evidence from different research studies on the same topic (Hyde & Grabe, 2008). As this shift has occurred, a heated debate has arisen over what constitutes a large, moderate, or small gender difference in meta-analytic results and what the implications of the magnitude of the difference are (e.g., Eagly, 1995, 2018; Hyde, 2005, 2014). On the one hand, Hyde (2005, p. 589) argued that most gender differences are in what may be considered a close-to-zero or small range, thereby supporting a "gender similarities" hypothesis over inflated claims of widespread gender differences. On the other hand, Eagly (1995) argued that a feminist political agenda devoted to disproving gender stereotypes has contributed to scholars' inaccurately minimizing gender differences and exaggerating gender similarities.

In response to this debate as it emerged, Martell et al. (1996) conducted a computer simulation that yielded intriguing results. They specified a hypothetical organization with eight hierarchical levels occupied by 500 employees at the bottom level, ten employees at the top level, and an equal number of women and men initially at each level. In this organization, consistent with meta-analytic findings that women's work is evaluated less favorably than men's work (Eagly et al., 1992), a performance evaluation system added "bias points" to the performance score of each male employee such that 1% of the variance in performance scores was attributable to gender. The simulation began with removing 15% of the jobholders at each level; open positions were then filled from within the organization by promoting candidates from the level below with the highest performance scores. Averaging across multiple simulation runs, even though half of the top-level positions were specified as filled by women at the onset, only 35% of top management positions were filled by women in the end. In other words, a slightly unequal playing field favoring men at the beginning of the simulation led to men holding almost two-thirds of top management positions by its end.

The simulation demonstrated that, as Martell and colleagues (1996, p. 158) put it, "a little bias hurt women a lot." The researchers concluded, "The effects of male-female differences are best determined not by the magnitude of the effect but its consequences in natural settings." Their study demonstrated the considerable practical importance of what may seem to be small gender differences, in this case a 1% difference favoring men in performance evaluation scores that influenced leader promotions. Even extremely small gender differences in a leadership-related phenomenon may have a cumulatively large effect over time, which in my opinion renders such differences definitely meaningful.

RESEARCHING GENDER AND LEADERSHIP: A PERSONAL JOURNEY

I began my doctoral studies in management and organizational behavior at the University of Massachusetts during the 1970s. A women's liberation movement that arose during the decade in nations such as the United Kingdom (Binard, 2017), the United States (Yelton-Stanley & Howard, 2000), and Australia (Magarey, 2018) had a major impact on women's attitudes, and indirectly men's attitudes, about their proper vis-à-vis preferred roles as well as on organizational and societal practices. To cite a few examples, pressure from this movement led to a greater awareness of and reduced emphasis on gender stereotypes in children's books, the elimination of separate advertising for "women's jobs" and "men's jobs" in newspapers, the passage of laws in many nations that banned discrimination on the basis of gender and other personal characteristics, and the appearance of women's studies (later called "gender studies") courses in many universities. Also during the 1970s, the proportion of women in managerial and professional occupations significantly increased (Powell, 1988). In short, it was a decade of considerable turmoil and change around gender issues.

I was influenced by these developments and sought to explore them in my research and teaching. My first research study on gender and leadership (Powell & Butterfield, 1979), to be described in Chapter 2, was conducted with Tony Butterfield, my former dissertation supervisor who became my life-long collaborator, colleague, mentor, and friend. At about the same time, early in my career at the University of Connecticut, I was given the opportunity to teach a graduate elective on any topic I wanted. I decided to teach a course with a unique title, "Women and Men in Management." The title was chosen to legitimize the course's having a male instructor (me), increase its appeal to male as well as female students, and call attention to the fact that people typically said "men and women" in that order rather than the order in the course title. To make a long story short, the course's first offering drew enough students for it to be offered on a regular basis; further, the course won the AACSB Committee on Equal Opportunity for Women Innovation Award, which inspired me to write a scholarly book with the same title "based on the award-winning course" (Sage, the publisher, was impressed).

What came to be the first edition of *Women and Men in Management* (Powell, 1988) chronicled the major transformations in the nature of female and male roles that had occurred in the workplace in recent years and looked ahead to what changes might be yet to come. It presented two diametrically opposed scenarios for the roles that women vis-à-vis men would play in the workplace of the future. In the positive scenario, all employees are treated according to the human capital they bring to the job – knowledge, skills, abilities, education, relevant work experience, past performance, and so on (Stumpf & London, 1981) – and given the chance to reach their leadership potential regardless of their gender. In the negative scenario, gender stereotypes and roles are the primary basis for treating others, predicting their behavior, and evaluating how they behave regardless of their human capital. The book concluded by basically saying "it's up to all of us" as to which scenario would be more likely to prevail in the future (Powell, 1988). However, given all the workplace changes that had occurred in the 1970s and 1980s, the overall message of the book was hopeful.

Since then, subsequent editions of *Women and Men in Management* (Powell, 1993, 2011, 2019; Powell & Graves, 2003) as well as subsequent articles in what came to be my research program on issues regarding gender and leadership have offered regular assessments of the state of affairs regarding these issues. However, as I have researched and written about this topic for over four decades, my perspective on these issues has gradually evolved from being more optimistic (e.g., "Sex discrimination in leadership positions favoring men has traditionally existed. However, there has recently been considerable growth in the proportion of women in management, a positive sign.") to being more pessimistic (e.g., "Sex discrimination in leadership positions favoring men persists, although its nature has evolved. Further, growth in the proportion of women in management, including in top management positions, has stalled.")

If the social goal of research on the linkage between gender and leadership is to eliminate the need for such research (i.e., to foster achievement of the positive scenario described above), I do not anticipate that this goal will be attained anytime in the foreseeable future.

Hence, this book. I believe that we still need to talk about the linkage between gender and leadership. Something troubling and problematic is still going on regarding this linkage that calls for our unwavering attention as scholars.

ORGANIZATION OF THE BOOK

The next four chapters of the book explore research questions regarding specific aspects of the linkage between gender and leadership. Chapter 2 addresses the frequently researched question, "Why do leader stereotypes emphasize masculinity?" Chapter 3 addresses a complementary question, "Why are there so few women in top management positions?" Chapter 4 addresses a question that has emerged in recent years, "Is there a female advantage or disadvantage in the managerial ranks?" Chapter 5 addresses a question ripped from today's headlines: "Why do (some) men in top management feel free to sexually harass women?"

The latter question is seldom addressed in the literature on the linkage between gender and leadership. However, I believe that it belongs in this book because it focuses on a type of behavior directed by mostly male leaders in positions with considerable power towards mostly lower-level female employees or job applicants with less power that is especially problematic, thereby rendering it a question pertaining to gender and leadership.

Chapter 6 serves as the concluding chapter of the book. It addresses the question, "What actions would work toward undoing the linkage between gender and leadership?" In raising this question, it responds to the notion that if social systems can become gendered or "do gender" (West & Zimmerman, 1987), they can also take steps toward "undoing gender" (Deutsch, 2007).

WHY DO LEADER STEREOTYPES EMPHASIZE MASCULINITY?

The linkage between gender and leader stereotypes has been one of the most researched topics in the field of gender and leadership. Research on the topic began in earnest in the 1970s, or at the time of the women's liberation movement that was exhibited in many nations (Binard, 2017; Magarey, 2018; Yelton-Stanley & Howard, 2000). Its purpose was to seek to explain why there were so few women in management positions worldwide (Powell, 1988). Although the proportion of female managers has increased in virtually all nations since those times (Powell & Graves, 2003), this linkage has continued to receive a considerable amount of scholarly attention; Koenig and colleagues (2011) conducted separate meta-analyses of research following different paradigms of the linkage that incorporated almost 200 effect sizes.

In this chapter, I first consider why gender stereotypes, leader stereotypes, and the linkage between them are important to examine. Next, I review the research into and theories of the linkage between gender and leader stereotypes, including my own research since the 1970s, followed by research with new results included and theories of change in this linkage. I conclude with the implications of the linkage for individuals who aspire to or already occupy leader roles.

STEREOTYPING

Stereotypes are defined as "beliefs about the characteristics, attributes, and behaviors of members of certain groups" (Hilton & von Hippel, 1996, p. 240). Stereotyping is a ubiquitous human phenomenon (Fiske, 1998), partly because stereotypes are so easy to use. When people are identifiable as members of a larger group, stereotyping makes it convenient for others to remember and categorize them. Stereotypes may be accurate or inaccurate, and positive or negative, in their depiction of the average group member. However, a stereotype of members of a particular group (e.g., women, men, leaders) is unlikely to characterize all group members accurately.

Stereotyping is a cognitive activity, related to learning (or imagining) and remembering distinctions between various groups of people. People who display prejudice, or a negative attitude toward members of other groups, are engaging in an emotional activity. Discrimination, a behavioral activity, is exhibited in how people treat and make decisions about members of other groups (Fiske, 1998). We have reason to be concerned about all three of these phenomena in the workplace. All of us may be targets of these phenomena, as well as engage in these phenomena. Further, negative stereotyping of members of a group may lead to prejudice and discrimination directed towards them. In this chapter, we focus on stereotyping on the basis of both gender and the leader role.

As noted in Chapter 1, *gender stereotypes* represent beliefs about the psychological traits that are characteristic of females vis-à-vis males. They are typically characterized by two independent dimensions, masculinity and femininity (Bem, 1974). According to gender stereotypes, males are high in "masculine" traits (also known as agentic traits) such as independence, aggressiveness, and dominance; in contrast, females are high in "feminine" traits (also known as communal traits) such as gentleness, sensitivity to the feelings of others, and tactfulness (Ellemers, 2018; Kite et al., 2008). Gender stereotypes may affect workplace outcomes by serving as the basis for differential treatment of and decisions about women vis-à-vis men solely because of their group membership (i.e., discrimination on the basis of gender) (Heilman, 2012; Koch et al., 2015; Perry et al., 1994).

The masculinity and femininity dimensions of gender stereotypes may be further divided into independent constructs; that is, there may be multiple masculinities and multiple femininities (Broadbridge & Simpson, 2011; Lewis, 2014). For example, masculinity may be subdivided into a personal dimension that focuses on independence and a social dimension that focuses on aggressiveness and dominance (Choi et al., 2009); further, there may be many variations of "hegemonic masculinity," or patterns of practices that go beyond stereotypes to maintain men's dominance over women (Connell & Messerschmidt, 2005). However, the terms masculinity and femininity refer to meaningful concepts for people and are an important part of their gender schemas (Bem, 1993). Thus, although the concepts themselves may be broken down further, I will refer to masculinity and femininity as global constructs in the book.

Gender stereotypes evoke strong reactions. For example, after the American Psychological Association (2018) issued its first-ever guidelines on counseling boys and men, some praised the guidelines as "reimagining boys in the 21st century" (Way, 2019, p. 926) while others criticized the guidelines as defining masculinity as an illness (Komisar, 2019). A poll of British young men found that although most had a negative view of masculinity, they felt pressured to "man up" by conforming to the male gender stereotype (Petter, 2018). Still others have argued that masculinity receives too much attention and the importance of "doing femininity" needs to be recognized (Fondas, 1997; Lewis, 2014).

Leader stereotypes represent beliefs about the traits that are characteristic of leaders or managers. In the leadership literature, leader stereotypes are often referred to as individuals' implicit leadership theories (Junker & van Dick, 2014), or beliefs about leadership in general. They evoke less strong reactions than gender stereotypes. However, they may also significantly affect workplace outcomes, in that candidates for selection or promotion who are stereotyped, whether accurately or not, as deficient in the traits needed for a specific leader position will be unlikely to attain the position.

If both gender and leader stereotypes have these kinds of effects, the linkage between the two types of stereotypes is likely to have significant effects as well. Hence, this chapter.

THE LINKAGE BETWEEN GENDER AND LEADER STEREOTYPES

Research

At the time I began my scholarly career, there had been little published research on the linkage between gender and leadership, and leadership theories had been based almost entirely on studies of male managers. A classic 1974 compendium of research results, *Handbook of Leadership* (Stogdill, 1974), discovered few studies that examined female leaders exclusively or even included female leaders in their samples. When female managers were present in organizations being studied, they were usually excluded from the analysis because their inclusion might lead to distorted results!

However, Bem (1974) had recently argued that more effective people are high in both masculine (agentic) and feminine (communal) traits, or "androgynous." Consistent with the feminist spirit of the time, the concept of androgyny received "instant celebrity" (Bem, 1993, p. 121) in the psychology of women literature. Androgyny was soon found to be associated with high self-esteem, a flexible response to situations rather than a rigid emphasis on feminine or masculine behaviors, and a host of other positive outcomes (Lenney, 1979). In short, androgyny was proposed as an ideal combination of "the best of both worlds." I found the concept appealing, as it was consistent with my own values ("let's get rid of expectations that people conform to gender stereotypes and roles if we can") and had apparent benefits.

When I first read Bem (1974), a light bulb went on in my head. I asked Tony Butterfield, "If the androgyny concept has not yet been applied in work settings, why not apply it ourselves?" As we later put it (Powell & Butterfield, 1979, p. 396), "If the more effective person is androgynous, the more effective *manager* may be androgynous as well." The proportion of women in management positions had been increasing, which may have contributed to the replacement of masculine standards for managerial behavior with androgynous standards. Accordingly, we optimistically hypothesized a linkage between gender and leader stereotypes such that the "good manager" would be perceived as androgynous (Powell & Butterfield, 1979). To test the hypothesis, we surveyed samples of undergraduate business students and part-time (i.e., evening) MBA students in the mid-1970s; respondents were asked to describe both themselves and a good manager on the Bem Sex-Role Inventory (BSRI; Bem, 1974), an instrument with separate scales assessing the independent dimensions of masculinity and femininity. Our hypothesis was soundly rejected. Instead, the good manager was perceived as possessing predominantly masculine traits by women and men in both populations.

Meanwhile, the proportion of women in management positions was continuing to rise (Powell, 1988). Also, in response to criticism of some of the items in the original BSRI, Bem had released a "new and improved" version of the BSRI, called the Short BSRI (Bem, 1981), that contained half of the original items and was found to be a more valid and reliable instrument (Choi et al., 2009). Therefore, we decided to survey the same two populations in the mid-1980s, now using the Short BSRI, while posing the same optimistic hypothesis: The good manager would be perceived as androgynous (Powell & Butterfield, 1989). In short, we were arguing that "we want a recount" of the earlier results with new data. Once again, the hypothesis was soundly rejected, both for the new data and for the earlier data re-analyzed using only the items included in the Short BSRI. The good manager was still perceived in predominantly masculine terms.

A decade later, Tony and I, this time with Jane Parent (Powell et al., 2002), revisited the linkage between gender and leader stereotypes with new data collected from the same two populations in the late 1990s. For this study, we got the message conveyed by our earlier results and reluctantly gave up on arguing for the applicability of the androgyny concept to descriptions of a good manager. Instead, because the proportion of women managers was still rising (Powell & Graves, 2003), we examined whether change in leader stereotypes in relation to gender stereotypes, perhaps due to this change in the composition of the managerial ranks, had occurred over time. Accordingly, we hypothesized that the good manager would be perceived in newly-collected data as less masculine than in data collected earlier. We found some support for this hypothesis for both undergraduate and part-time MBA students. However, the good manager was still described in predominantly masculine terms as before.

In our next study in this stream of research, incorporating data collected from identical populations in the late 2000s with data collected during the three previous decades, Tony and I decided to examine stability and change in the correspondence between self-descriptions and good-manager descriptions over four decades (Powell & Butterfield, 2015a). We found that, when good-manager descriptions and self-descriptions were compared, men consistently saw themselves as more like the good manager than women did in data collected in each decade and for all four decades combined. There was no consistent pattern of change for either women or men in correspondence between self- and good-manager descriptions across the four decades. Also, as before, the good manager was seen as possessing predominantly masculine traits.

We have extended this stream of research over time to the political arena. Periodically, during US presidential election campaigns, we have collected similar data using the Short BSRI (Bem, 1981) on descriptions of the "ideal president" as well as the candidates of the two major political parties (e.g., Powell & Butterfield, 2011; Powell et al., 2018). In such studies, we have always found that the ideal president is described in predominantly masculine terms. Also, the candidate whose leader profile is perceived as closest to that of the ideal president typically, but not always, wins the election; Donald Trump's victory over Hillary Clinton in 2016 was the exception (Powell et al., 2018).

Considerable research by others has followed Powell and Butterfield's (1979) original research design in examining the linkage between gender and leader stereotypes. For example, additional supporting evidence has been found within specific occupations such as the military ("think military leader – think masculine;" Boyce & Herd, 2003) and athletics ("think athletic director – think masculine;" Burton et al., 2009). As summarized in Koenig et al. (2011), these research results offer strong support for what I call the *think manager – think masculine* paradigm of the linkage between gender and leader stereotypes (they called it the "agency – communion paradigm").

Schein (1973, 1975) initiated a related stream of research in the 1970s. She compiled a list of characteristics that people commonly believed distinguished between women and men, i.e., served as the basis for gender stereotypes. She then asked a sample of US middle managers to describe how well each of the characteristics fit women in general, men in general, or successful middle managers in general. Schein hypothesized that because the vast majority of managers were men, the managerial job would be regarded as requiring personal attributes thought to be more characteristic of men than women. In support of her hypothesis, she found that both male and female middle managers believed that a successful middle manager possessed personal characteristics that more closely matched beliefs about the characteristics of men in general than those of women in general. In subsequent studies conducted worldwide, both men and women believe that men are more similar to successful managers than women are, but men endorse such beliefs to a greater extent than women do (Schein et al., 1996). As summarized in Koenig et al. (2011), these results support the *think manager – think male* paradigm of the linkage between gender and leader stereotypes, especially among men.

Thus the linkage between gender and leader stereotypes continues to reflect the closely related notions of think manager – think masculine and think manager – think male. If men are perceived as essentially masculine as a group as gender stereotypes suggest (Ellemers, 2018; Kite et al., 2008), the two paradigms similarly demonstrate the overall masculinity of leader stereotypes (Koenig et al., 2011). At the same time, my initial optimism (and hopefulness) that leader stereotypes would emphasize androgyny rather than masculinity as more women entered the managerial ranks has evolved over time towards pessimism. If androgyny theories originating with Bem (1974) have not helped to explain the linkage between gender and leader stereotypes, we need to turn to other theories.

Theories

Many theories have been offered to explain the emphasis on masculinity in leader stereotypes. According to social-system-centered theories, patriarchal social systems in which the male has power and authority over the female have almost always prevailed throughout recorded history (Alvesson & Due Billing, 2009; Calás et al., 2014; Maier, 1999; Marshall, 1984). Because social systems are essentially gendered in and of themselves (Acker, 1990; Calás &

Smircich, 1996; Ridgeway, 1991; Risman, 2004; West & Zimmerman, 1987), gendered processes in societies enacted in organizations dictate the enactment of power and authority, including what behaviors leaders are allowed to exhibit (Broadbridge & Hearn, 2008).

For example, consider the concept of hierarchy, a familiar organizational structure in which every entity (person or work unit) except one is subordinate to a sole other entity. This structure, which represents a situation-centered factor, is consistent with men's greater display of dominance, a masculine trait in gender stereotypes. However, the establishment of hierarchies is reinforced by gendered processes in patriarchal social systems (Acker, 1990). Hierarchies enable employees in higher-level positions, whomever they may be, to dominate employees in lower-level positions. Thus hierarchies may have become the prevalent organizational form because they were designed by men to favor leaders who possess a trait (dominance) associated with men. Alternative organizational forms such as a web structure (in which the manager is a central coordinator more than a controller) or hub structure (in which all employees' work is interconnected; Mintzberg & Van der Hayden, 1999) place less emphasis on masculine behaviors and have been less acknowledged in leadership theories.

According to role congruity theory (Eagly & Karau, 2002), the linkage between widely held gender and leader stereotypes that represent social system factors puts female leaders at a disadvantage by forcing them to deal with the perceived incongruity between the leader role and their gender role. If women display predominantly feminine characteristics, they fail to meet the requirements of the leader role. However, if women display predominantly masculine characteristics, they fail to meet the requirements of the female gender role. In contrast, because the leader role and the male gender role are perceived as congruent, men's legitimacy as leaders is not questioned. Due to the perceived incongruity between the leader role and the female gender role, women are less likely to see themselves as good managers than men do, a research finding reported earlier (Powell & Butterfield, 2015a).

Status characteristics theory (Ridgeway, 1991, 2006), a social-system-centered theory, argues that women's presence in leader positions violates the societal norm of men's higher status and superiority. Because of their weaker status position in society, women are required to monitor others' reactions to themselves and be responsive to interpersonal cues, leading them to specialize in feminine or communal traits. In contrast, because of their stronger status position in society, men get more opportunities to initiate actions and influence decision-making, leading them to specialize in masculine or agentic traits.

The lack of fit model (Heilman, 1983, 2012) represents a person-centered theory that focuses on decision-makers' cognitive processes. When decision makers believe that men possess the traits that are best suited for leader roles in greater abundance than women, their judgments and decisions are likely to be biased, leading them to evaluate male candidates as representing a better "fit" for such roles than female candidates regardless of their human capital. As a result, when employers select or promote candidates who fit a gender-based prototype for leader roles (Perry et al., 1994), those candidates who are judged by decision-makers to offer a lesser fit (i.e., women) are less likely to attain the leader positions being filled.

All of these theories argue that the linkage between gender and leader stereotypes exerts a powerful influence on beliefs about who belongs in leader roles (men) and who does not (women). They represent only a sample of the theories that have been offered to explain the linkage. However, they convey a consistent message.

In summary, research results from studies following different paradigms and theories seeking to explain these results have generally concluded that leader stereotypes emphasize masculine traits, or those associated in gender stereotypes more with men than women. The next section of the chapter addresses whether the emphasis on masculinity in leader stereotypes has changed over time, and, if so, why.

HAS THE LINKAGE BETWEEN GENDER AND LEADER STEREOTYPES CHANGED OVER TIME?

Research

Gender stereotypes have been generally stable over the past five decades (Broverman et al., 1972; Haines et al., 2016). That is, there has been relatively little change in beliefs about the traits of the typical male (masculine) vis-à-vis the typical female (feminine). According to the most recent results (Eagly et al., 2020), men are seen as just as masculine or agentic as ever, and women are seen as more feminine or communal than ever. This stability in gender stereotypes begs the question, "If gender stereotypes have not changed over time, what about the linkage between gender and leader stereotypes?"

To address this question, I re-analyzed combined data from my four previous studies of descriptions of a good manager described earlier (Powell & Butterfield, 1979, 1989, 2015a; Powell et al., 2002) for the purposes of this book to examine trends over four decades. In the new analysis, I followed Powell and Butterfield's (1979) four-quadrant classification scheme for individuals' good-manager descriptions based on their masculinity and femininity good-manager scores on the Short BSRI (Bem, 1981): androgynous (high in masculinity and femininity), masculine (high in masculinity and low in femininity), feminine (low in masculinity and high in femininity), or undifferentiated (low in masculinity and femininity). Data from different samples at each of four points in time, from women and men, and from undergraduate business students and part-time MBA students, were weighted equally to prevent larger subsamples from exercising greater influence over the results than smaller subsamples.

The results of this analysis indicated that the proportion of survey respondents who described a good manager as masculine decreased over time from 61% to 50%, a significant decline. The androgynous proportion also significantly decreased from 27% to 19%, the feminine proportion stayed steady at 2–5%, and the undifferentiated proportion significantly increased from 10% to 27%. Thus, although the masculine proportion decreased over time, it remained the largest proportion by far, whereas the feminine proportion remained the smallest by far. Consistent with this trend, the difference between masculinity and femininity good-manager scores favoring masculinity significantly decreased over time.

Koenig and colleagues (2011) also examined differences over time between masculinity and femininity leader scores in studies that followed the think manager – think masculine paradigm inspired by Powell & Butterfield (1979) or the think manager – think male paradigm inspired by Schein (1973, 1975). In studies following each of these paradigms, they found that differences between masculinity and femininity leader scores favoring masculinity significantly decreased over time.

In summary, research results suggest that, although gender stereotypes have tended to be stable, leader stereotypes have become decreasingly masculine over time, although they still emphasize masculine over feminine traits. Next, I consider possible explanations for this trend as well as for the continued overall emphasis on masculinity in leader stereotypes.

Theories

All stereotypes, including gender and leader stereotypes, tend to be durable over time (Hilton & von Hippel, 1996). This is because they are reinforced by both cognitive and social processes. Regarding cognitive processes, individuals tend to categorize people into groups and then develop beliefs about the attributes held in common by members of different groups, including their own (Tajfel & Turner, 1986); these beliefs in turn act as self-fulfilling prophecies – instances in which expectations cause behaviors that make the expectations come true (Eden, 2003). Regarding social processes, individuals learn stereotypes of different groups during their early gender socialization experiences from parents, teachers, and other significant adults in their lives as well as from the popular media (Martin & Ruble, 2009; Powell, 2019).

Stereotypes may also change over time (Hilton & von Hippel, 1996). Rothbart (1981) distinguished between two theoretical models of stereotype change, the bookkeeping model and the conversion model. According to the bookkeeping model, stereotypes are constantly open to gradual revision as new pieces of information, either confirming or disconfirming, are received. According to the conversion model, stereotypes change suddenly in response to highly salient and critical pieces of disconfirming information. The bookkeeping model is "deliberate, methodical, and predictable" in nature, whereas the conversion model is "somewhat erratic, impulsive, and unpredictable" (Rothbart, 1981, p. 176). If new information about the accuracy of a given stereotype is moderately disconfirming, the bookkeeping model would predict moderate change in it and the conversion model would predict no change. However, if new information overwhelmingly discredits the stereotype, both models would predict substantial change in it.

Thus, there are theoretical reasons for why gender and leader stereotypes may have changed over time. The key determinant of whether a stereotype actually changes according to Rothbart (1981) is whether there has been sufficient disconfirming information to trigger change according to either the bookkeeping or the conversion model.

Chapter 1 described the onset of a period of considerable social change in the 1970s, roughly five decades ago. The changes that have occurred since then in women's educational attainment in preparation for managerial and professional careers and in their workplace status have been pronounced (Powell, 2019; Powell & Butterfield, 2015a). The level of gender segregation of occupations has dropped in most nations since the 1970s, primarily due to the increased employment of women in male-dominated occupations (Powell, 2019; Seron et al., 2016). Overall, the level of societal change that has occurred over the last five decades would seem sufficient enough to promote change in both gender and leader stereotypes according to Rothbart's (1981) bookkeeping and conversion models of stereotype change.

Yet gender stereotypes have exhibited relatively little change (Broverman et al., 1972; Eagly et al., 2020; Haines et al., 2016). How may the general stability in gender stereotypes be explained? Increases in women's educational attainment and workplace status according to indicators such as their labor force participation rate and their proportion of the labor force and managerial positions seem to have mostly stalled or slightly reversed direction during the 21st century so far; most of the changes in women's status over the last five decades actually occurred during the last three decades of the 20th century (Powell, 2019; Powell & Butterfield 2015a). Eagly and colleagues (2020) suggested that this may be because women tend to enter the labor force by assuming existing or newly-created jobs that call for more feminine or communal qualities than other jobs, even within male-dominated occupations. Gender segregation in the workplace may also be resilient due to continued gender segregation within households, with women performing or being responsible for most of the housework in heterosexual households (Breen & Cooke, 2005; Warren, 2011) even when they earn more than their male partners (Lyonette & Crompton, 2015). These factors may have contributed to maintaining gender stereotypes despite the overall increase in women's societal status over the last five decades.

However, given the same set of factors, leader stereotypes have changed somewhat, so that they now place less emphasis on masculinity in the past. What else might be operating that would allow for modest change in leader stereotypes? In recent decades, new theories of effective leadership have emerged that place greater emphasis on feminine traits associated with women than earlier theories based primarily on observations of male leaders (Powell & Butterfield, 2015a; Stogdill, 1974). For example, there has been an explosion of interest since the 1990s in theories of transformational leadership (Bass, 1985), a leadership style that has been more associated with the female than the male gender stereotype (Bass et al., 1996; Kark, 2004). In the same vein, Alimo-Metcalfe (2010) found support for an essentially feminine model of inclusive leadership. Further, best-selling books on management have tended to emphasize traits and behaviors associated more with women than men, thereby contributing to what Fondas (1997, p. 257) called the "feminization" of management. These factors may have been sufficient to promote a gradual change in leader stereotypes de-emphasizing masculinity that is consistent with Rothbart's (1981) bookkeeping model of stereotype change, but insufficient to eliminate the overall emphasis on masculinity in leader stereotypes that would be consistent with the conversion model of stereotype change.

CONCLUSIONS

The linkage between gender and leader stereotypes emphasizing masculinity has significant implications, especially for people who aspire to or already hold leadership positions. It places women at a disadvantage compared to men with equivalent credentials and experience, because the perceived incongruity or lack of fit between the leader role and women's gender role fosters their legitimacy as leaders being questioned (Eagly & Karau, 2002; Heilman, 1983, 2012; Perry et al., 1994). As a result, women are less likely to perceive themselves as good leaders than men do (Powell & Butterfield, 2015a), which may make them less likely than men to develop their managerial skills, pursue careers in the managerial ranks, or pursue careers in the *top* managerial ranks (Heilman, 2012).

When women assume leader roles, leader stereotypes act as constraints on their behavior. Many organizations exert strong pressure on their members to conform to standards of behavior dictated by those in positions of power and authority. As long as men remain in the majority in top management ranks and increases in women's status in the 21st century remain stalled (Powell, 2019; Powell & Butterfield, 2015a), the masculine leader stereotype is likely to prevail, and female leaders will be expected to behave as male leaders. In this way, a leader stereotype emphasizing masculinity becomes a self-fulfilling prophecy (Eden, 2003).

However, leader stereotypes do not necessarily apply to the actual practice of management. As noted earlier, stereotypes of all kinds tend to be durable and may not reflect current realities. Stereotypes of leaders as possessing predominantly masculine traits may not reflect what actually makes for effective leaders. Instead, these stereotypes may reflect only that most managers have been men and that most men have been expected to conform to a norm of masculinity.

Further, leader stereotypes may be dependent on the racial and ethnic composition of the management ranks. The vast majority of both female and male managers, especially at top management levels, are whites, with women of color being the most underrepresented group (Piazza, 2016). Leader stereotypes may largely reflect beliefs about the characteristics of leaders from the dominant racial and ethnic group in the managerial ranks and ignore the characteristics of leaders from other groups (Parker & ogilvie, 1996; Sanchez-Hucles & Davis, 2010).

In conclusion, I expect that the linkage between gender and leader stereotypes is likely to continue to emphasize masculinity, even if there are gradual declines in this emphasis. I see the emphasis on masculinity in leader stereotypes as unlikely to go away entirely, at least anytime soon, because the forces that maintain it are so strong. Further, it is likely to be reinforced by the continued predominance of men in top management positions, which leads us to the next chapter.

3

WHY ARE THERE SO FEW WOMEN IN TOP MANAGEMENT POSITIONS?

The first female chief executive officer (CEO) of a Financial Times Stock Exchange (FTSE, or "Footsie") 100 company, consisting of the top 100 companies by market capitalization listed on the London Stock Exchange, was appointed in 1997. At the time of writing, there are six female CEOs in the FTSE 100 (Ball, 2019). What should be made of this trend? It depends on what statistic is used to describe it. On the one hand, there has been a 500% increase (from 1% to 6%) in the proportion of female CEOs of FTSE 100 companies over the last twenty-plus years, which may seem like a large increase. On the other hand, during the same period, the proportion of male FTSE 100 CEOs decreased from 99% to 94%, a 5% decline, which hardly seems large at all. There are currently more FTSE 100 CEOs named "Steve" than there are female CEOs, and there is a tie with the number of FTSE 100 CEOs named "Dave" (Ball, 2019).

Across the pond, there was one female CEO of a Fortune 500 company, consisting of the top 500 US companies by total revenue, in 1996 (Pew Research Center, 2015). Currently, 33 of the Fortune 500 CEOs are female (Zillman, 2019). Thus, the increase in the proportion of female CEOs of Fortune 500 corporations over a 20+-year period has been 32,000% (from 0.2% to 6.6%), certainly a large proportion. However, the decrease in the proportion of male Fortune 500 CEOs over about the same period of time has been only 6.4% (from 99.8% to 93.4%), or similar to the decrease in the proportion of male FTSE 100 CEOs.

What do these trends in the proportion of female CEOs in large companies really mean? Not surprisingly, there are different perspectives. For example, when the proportion of female Fortune 500 CEOs reached 4.0% for the first time, this achievement was heralded as signaling "the dawn of the age of female CEOs" (Parker, 2013). However, others have argued that there are still not enough female CEOs (Brooke-Marciniak & Schreiber, 2015) and that views of increased gender parity in the top management ranks represent "delusions of progress" (Carter & Silva, 2010). My perspective is that these trends have not significantly changed the reality that there are still very few, in my opinion *too* few, women in top management positions.

The low proportion of women in top management positions has been attributed to what has been called the "glass ceiling" phenomenon (Davidson & Cooper, 1992; Powell, 1999; Powell & Butterfield, 1994, 2015b). The glass ceiling is defined as "a transparent barrier that (keeps) women from rising above a certain level" (Morrison et al., 1987, p. 13). The term is primarily used to refer to women's restricted access to top management levels, although glass ceilings can exist at any managerial level. According to the glass ceiling metaphor, success consists of climbing to the peak of a mountain, and impediments to success consist of transparent, invisible ceilings that block or limit access to the peak for women as a group; as a result of glass ceilings, women can see the mountain peak, but they face greater obstacles than men as a group in attaining it (Sleek, 2015). Similar metaphors include a concrete ceiling (for women of color), a marble ceiling (for women in government), a sticky floor, glass chain, and labyrinth (Arifeen & Gatrell, 2020; Carli & Eagly, 2016; Piazza, 2016; Smith et al., 2012). In the book, I use the term "glass ceiling" because it has been the most popular term to refer to barriers to women's attaining top management positions.

Glass ceilings are troubling and problematic. First, they are problematic from an organizational effectiveness perspective. It is not exactly a smart human resources practice for organizations to artificially restrict the candidate pool for promotions to top management on the basis of gender, race, ethnicity, sexual orientation, or any other job-irrelevant personal characteristic. Organizations that do so would seem likely to be less effective at attracting and retaining managerial talent than organizations that take fuller advantage, and better care, of all of the human resources available to them (Powell & Butterfield, 2015b).

Second, glass ceilings are problematic from an organizational justice perspective. Organizational justice theories (Greenberg, 1990) suggest that employees are concerned with both procedural justice (i.e., whether the means by which personnel decisions such as promotion decisions and performance appraisals are made about them are fair) and distributive justice (i.e., whether the outcomes of personnel decisions made about them are fair). Regarding procedural justice, it is unjust for women as a group to have their membership in this group taken into account to their disadvantage, whether consciously or unconsciously, in decision-making procedures involving promotions to top management positions. Regarding distributive justice, it is unjust for women as a group to have their managerial advancement restricted simply because of their membership in this group (Powell & Butterfield, 2015b).

Moreover, it is important for organizations to be seen as fair in their personnel procedures and outcomes. Women perceive the existence of a glass ceiling that restricts their advancement to top management to a greater extent than men do, with such perceptions contributing to lower perceptions of distributive justice and greater intentions to quit their job (Foley et al., 2002). Perceptions of a glass ceiling to women's disadvantage may have a substantial negative impact on an organization's success in attracting, engaging, and retaining female managerial talent, which in turn restricts its effectiveness (Powell & Butterfield, 2015b).

In this chapter, I first review person-centered, situation-centered, and social-system-centered theories that have been offered for why there are so few women in top management positions. Next, I revisit an empirical field study conducted with Tony Butterfield on the glass ceiling phenomenon (Powell & Butterfield, 1994), the results of which suggested actions that organizations may take to work towards shattering their glass ceilings and increasing the numbers of women in top management positions. Finally, I reconsider the merits of the study's implications for practice almost three decades later. As we consider the question in the chapter title, one thing is clear. It is *not* simply a matter of time until women assume their fair share of these positions – something has to change.

THEORIES OF THE GLASS CEILING PHENOMENON

Person-centered theories

Horner (1972) proposed an early person-centered theory by advocating the existence of a fundamental personality characteristic, the "fear of success," among women as a group. She argued that traits required for success in achieving career goals (e.g., independent, competitive, has leadership potential) are inconsistent with the feminine gender stereotype (i.e., traits associated with females) and more consistent with the masculine gender stereotype (i.e., traits associated with males; Ellemers, 2018; Kite et al., 2008). As a result, when women anticipate that the probability of their achieving a career goal such as attaining a top management position is high, they experience anxieties activated by a motive to avoid success that keeps them from pursuing the goal. In contrast, men as a group experience no such anxieties and display no such motive. However, undermining the theory's validity, Horner's (1972) supporting research for the fear of success concept was found to have major methodological flaws (Levine & Crumrine, 1975). Further, a fear of success could be a response to situational or social system factors rather than an individual motive.

Another early person-centered theory proposed that men emerge from their childhood and adolescence as better prepared to be managers than women. Hennig & Jardim (1977, p. 63) argued that men "bring to the management setting a clearer, stronger and more definite understanding of where they see themselves going, what they will have to do, how they will have to act, and what they must take into account if they are to achieve the objectives they set for themselves." They attributed the gender difference in preparation for managerial roles to males' greater participation in competitive sports than that of girls during their formative years (Deaner & Smith, 2012). However, Hennig & Jardim (1977) argued that women managers may acquire the skills needed to advance in organizational hierarchies to top management positions.

Other early person-centered explanations reviewed by Marshall (1984) for why there are so few women in top management positions include that women have less motivation to manage then men, that women believe stereotypes about themselves as unfit to manage and act accordingly, and that women's inclusion in the top management ranks causes societal harm because their children, husbands, and homes inevitably suffer. Marshall's (1984, p. 40) exasperation upon reviewing the evidence for such theories, which she concluded were dubious as a whole, was clear: "I have had enough." Overall, person-centered theories have been largely discredited by scholars since Riger and Galligan (1980) first classified them as such (Powell & Butterfield, 2015b). Nonetheless, they retain an enduring appeal for some observers.

For example, the "opt-out revolution" has become a well-known phenomenon in recent years, at least in the popular media (Belkin, 2003; Kuperberg & Stone, 2008). According to media reports, educated women are increasingly choosing to opt out of careers that place them on the fast track to top management because of parenthood or other personal reasons. Scholars have exhibited varying reactions to this media-driven, person-centered explanation for the low representation of women in top management positions.

Mainiero and Sullivan (2006) argued that rather than women lacking aspirations to top management, potential top executives' choices to opt out may represent a reaction to extreme organizational expectations for their work hours and time. Managers are increasingly being pressured by their employers to work as much time as possible (Milliken & Dunn-Jensen, 2005). Because of improvements in electronic technologies, managers find it difficult or impossible to turn off work when they are technically "at home" but digitally tethered to work (Ferguson et al., 2016); in effect, they feel compelled to "sleep with their smartphone" (Perlow, 2012). Being available at all times is regarded as demonstrating high commitment to the organization and job, which is essential to being considered for a top-management position. An organizational culture that emphasizes long work hours and 24/7 availability represents a situation-centered explanation for what has been described as a person-centered phenomenon.

In the same vein, Kossek et al. (2017) questioned whether women were "opting out," a person-centered explanation, or "pushed out," a situation-centered explanation. Hoobler et al. (2014) suggested that when women do not aspire to managerial careers, it is because of managers' biased evaluations of them as less career-motivated than men, which hinders their development and suppresses their aspirations for top management positions, also a situation-centered explanation. Harman & Sealy (2017) proposed that, rather than women opting out due to a lack of ambition, their self-efficacy or belief in their ability to achieve their goals (a personal factor) interacts with whether their organizational context is positive or negative (a situational factor) to influence their path forward, either to opt in and pursue their ambition within the organization or to leave to fulfill their ambition elsewhere.

Finally, Tony Butterfield and I (2013) found that female and male business students did not differ in aspirations to top management. Instead, those who described themselves as possessing a higher level of masculine traits were more likely to aspire (i.e., "opt in") to top management. Thus, contrary to media accounts of an opt-out revolution for educated women, we offered an alternative person-centered explanation for why educated individuals would opt in or out of careers aimed at attaining top management positions (Powell & Butterfield, 2013).

Further, a small but growing genre of best-selling books has emerged by celebrity women executives and business owners ("female heroes;" Adamson & Kelan, 2019) such as Sheryl Sandberg (2013) and Karren Brady (2012). Such books typically offer accounts of how the authors have achieved success, despite all the challenges faced, in all facets of life and recommendations for how other women may do the same. The books share common features: they are authored by women who became celebrities through their business activities, they are autobiographical, and they discuss how the authors have simultaneously experienced (and other women may experience) motherhood, business success, and work–family balance. Overall, such books have been argued to reflect a postfeminist sensibility by focusing on person-centered solutions to gender inequalities that women face; in other words, they are "calling on women to change themselves to succeed" (Adamson & Kelan, 2019, p. 981).

In particular, Sandberg's *Lean In: Women, Work, and the Will to Lead* (2013) has been a best-seller since it was published and has inspired the creation of "Lean In Circles" in which women meet regularly to work on new skills, network, and support each other. The book offers many suggestions for women to keep from holding themselves back in their careers, some of which are supported by research evidence and others of which are not (Chrobot-Mason et al., 2019). Sandberg's (2013) critics have accused her of perpetuating a "fix the women" focus (Metz & Kumra, 2019) or being naive by advocating that women should "lean in" to be successful in their careers (Newman, 2018); it might also be beneficial for women's success in life if men were to "lean out" (Whippman, 2019).

In conclusion, it seems likely that person-centered theories and explanations for women's low representation in the ranks of top management will continue to be popular among some observers, regarded as problematic by other observers, and subjected to critical examination by scholars on a lagged basis for the foreseeable future.

Situation-centered theories

Situation-centered theories and explanations for why there are so few women in top management positions primarily focus on the organizational contexts experienced by women who aspire to or may be considered for top management positions. These situations are influenced by decisions about exactly who is promoted to such positions when openings arise, and they are also influenced by the organizational contexts in which such decisions are made. In this section, we consider decision-makers' cognitive processes as situational factors that may contribute to gender discrimination favoring male candidates for top management positions as well as the organizational contexts in which such discrimination occurs.

Decisions about who occupies top management positions are more likely to be influenced by decision-makers' cognitive processes than decisions about lower-level managerial positions. The higher the position within the managerial ranks, the less the importance of "objective" credentials such as education and training (Antal & Krebsbach-Gnath, 1988). As a result, women's increased educational attainment over the last five decades (Powell, 2019) has had a greater effect on hiring and promotion into entry-level management positions than on promotions to top management. The effect of decision-makers' biases and stereotypes is likely to be greater when there is less reliance on objective credentials and more reliance on "subjective" factors such as perceived fit.

Decision-makers' endorsement of leader stereotypes is likely to influence the proportion of women in top management. If leader stereotypes are masculine ("think manager – think masculine") and favor men for managerial positions in general ("think manager – think male") as Chapter 2 demonstrated, stereotypes of *top* managers are also likely to emphasize masculinity and favor male candidates, thereby reinforcing the low proportion of women in top management.

Perry et al. (1994) noted that individual decision-makers develop a schema or mental model about the attributes of jobholders that influences their hiring and promotion decisions. A schema may be either gender-based, incorporating the gender of jobholders in some way, or gender-neutral, ignoring the gender of jobholders. Gender is most likely to be incorporated into decision-makers' jobholder schemas when persons primarily of a particular gender occupy the job under consideration (Perry et al., 1994), which is certainly the case for top management positions. Thus, as the lack of fit model (Heilman, 1983, 2012) described in Chapter 2 would predict, women tend to be regarded as providing a lesser fit with the demands of top management positions than men do. In the same vein, as role congruity theory (Eagly & Karau, 2002), also described in Chapter 2, would predict, the top manager role is seen as less congruent with the female than the male gender role, which of course benefits male candidates.

In a classic study, Kanter (1977, p. 63) characterized the results of such decision-making processes as "homosocial reproduction." She argued that the primary motivation in organizational bureaucracies is to minimize uncertainty in decision-making. Uncertainty is present whenever individuals are relied upon, and the effects of such uncertainty are greatest when these individuals hold significant responsibility for the direction of the organization, such as top executives. One way to minimize uncertainty in the executive suite is to close top management positions to people who are regarded as "different." Thus, women have a difficult time in entering top management positions because they are seen as posing too much uncertainty by male decision-makers (Kanter, 1977). Theories of homophily, or the tendency and preference for people to associate with similar others (McPherson et al., 2001), provide a further explanation for why overwhelmingly male decision-makers overwhelmingly choose male candidates for top management positions.

Decision-makers' perceptions of the effects of senior-level women's versus senior-level men's hormones is an example of a situation-centered explanation that focuses on biological forces. Decision-makers for promotions to top management may perceive senior-level women as governed by fluctuating hormones throughout and beyond their reproductive years, indicating their lack of competence to make rational decisions required of a top executive (Gatrell et al., 2017). In contrast, senior-level men's hormones are assumed to be less problematic. The perceived linkage between "reproductivity and productivity" represents a barrier to women attaining top management positions that contributes to gender discrimination. It reflects a general discomfort with female bodies in the workplace (Gatrell, 2013), in this case in top management positions (Gatrell et al., 2017).

The existence of *glass walls*, which are the result of past decisions about who fills different types of lower-level managerial positions, may influence who is in the best position to rise to the top management ranks. Line functions (e.g., production, sales, research and development) are more central to the provision of organizational products and services, whereas staff functions (e.g., human resources, corporate communications, public relations) are more peripheral to the provision of products and services. As a result, managerial jobs in line functions confer higher status and provide greater developmental opportunities that prepare individuals to assume top management responsibilities than managerial jobs in staff functions (Baron et al., 1986). Reflecting the existence of glass walls, female managers tend to be concentrated in staff functions, whereas male managers tend to be concentrated in line functions. Further, within staff functions, female managers are less likely than male managers to move into line functions (Lyness & Schrader, 2006). Glass walls provide a further situation-centered explanation for glass ceilings: because middle- and lower-level female managers are concentrated in staff functions with limited developmental opportunities, they are less likely than male managers to attain top management positions.

Decision-makers may also take into account the nature of the top-management position they are filling. Theories of *glass cliffs* address the question, "When women attain top management positions, where do they find themselves?" The answer is, "They find themselves in precarious leader positions" (Mulcahy & Linehan, 2014; Ryan & Haslam, 2005; Ryan et al., 2016). That is, the traditional "think manager – think male" association documented in Chapter 2 is weakened during times of poor organizational performance and replaced by a "think crisis – think female" association (Ryan et al., 2011). As a result, female CEOs experience greater pressures than their male counterparts from the onset of their terms. They come under greater threat from activist investors (Gupta et al., 2018), have shorter tenure in the position (Glass & Cook, 2016), and are more likely to be fired even when their firm is performing well (Gupta et al., 2020). Glass cliffs represent a second wave of gender discrimination that occurs as (some) women break through glass ceilings (Ryan & Haslam, 2005).

Consistent with glass cliff theories, women and men of color as well as white women tend to be promoted to more precarious CEO positions than white men. Further, when firm performance declines during their tenure as CEO, they tend to be replaced by white men, which has been dubbed the "savior effect" (Cook & Glass, 2014, p. 1080). Thus, an intersectional perspective (Acker, 2006; Ridgeway & Kricheli-Katz, 2013; Rodriguez et al., 2016; Rosette et al., 2018; Smooth, 2010) is necessary when considering glass cliffs and other situation-centered explanations for the status of women as well as racial and ethnic minorities in top management.

Finally, female decision-makers who have broken through glass ceilings may use particular cognitive processes and behaviors to hold back lower-level women who might be future candidates for top management positions. Mavin and her colleagues (e.g., Mavin, 2006a, 2006b; Mavin et al., 2014) have examined psychological "micro-violence" in women's intra-gender relations. Women in top management may exhibit intra-gender micro-violence across organizational levels by distancing themselves from and hindering the advancement of lower-level women (Mavin et al., 2014). Whereas early, media-driven usage of the "queen bee" metaphor (Staines et al., 1973) blamed top-level women for blocking the advancement of lower-level women (Derks et al., 2016; Ellemers et al., 2012), Mavin et al. (2014, p. 441) blamed gendered social systems in which women in top management feel compelled to "ventriloquize patriarchal attitudes." Thus, individual women's rising above a glass ceiling may contribute to keeping other women below it, which also represents a second wave of gender discrimination.

Although the situation-centered theories and explanations reviewed disagree on the underlying rationale, they agree that women tend to be discriminated against when decisions are made for promotions to top management. However, gender discrimination is not necessarily intentional (Motowidlo, 1986);

decision-makers may be unaware of how their gender schemas (Bem, 1993) affect their decisions about top management positions. Unconscious cognitive processes, including decision-makers' leader stereotypes, preferences for similar others, beliefs about hormonal influences, assignments of managers to line vs. staff functions, assessments of the fit of candidates for top management positions depending on the precariousness of the position, and other factors reflecting their gender schemas, may lead to their making biased judgments that result in gender discrimination favoring men.

Social-system-centered theories

Social-system-centered theories and explanations for why there are so few women in top management positions primarily focus on gendered processes at the social system or societal level. These processes may influence the organizational contexts in which decisions about who attains top management positions are made. They may also influence individuals' aspirations to top management and supporting behaviors as well as decision-makers' selection decisions about who attains top management positions. Overall, social-system-centered theories may at least partially explain both situation-centered and person-centered phenomena that contribute to there being few women in top management positions.

Social-system-centered theories have a common focus on the macro-level processes by which social systems become gendered (e.g., Acker, 1990; Calás & Smircich, 1996; Ely & Padavic, 2007; Lorber, 1994; Marshall, 1984; Ridgeway, 1991; Risman, 2004; West & Zimmerman, 1987). Feminist theories provide particularly rich theoretical perspectives on the gendering of social systems. There have been many classifications of feminist theories (e.g., Ahl, 2006; Calás & Smircich, 1996; Greer & Greene, 2003). For example, Calás & Smircich (1996) distinguished between liberal, radical, psychoanalytic, Marxist, socialist, poststructuralist, and Third World/(post)colonial feminist theories. However, a common theme of most social-system-centered theories, including feminist theories, is that male dominance is manifested throughout social systems, including in organizational hierarchies (Acker, 1990), and that this domination is problematic (Calás & Smircich, 1996).

West & Zimmerman (1987, p. 129), in one of the most cited and influential articles in the field of sociology and gender studies (Jurik & Siemsen, 2009), argued that "gender is not a set of traits, nor a variable, nor a role, but the product of social doings." Doing gender is manifested in everyday social interactions that may seem natural but are actually scripted by gendered social systems. In turn, the gendering of social systems contributes to the establishment of gender differences among people that would not otherwise exist. In a later commentary on their seminal article, West & Zimmerman (2009, p. 117) added that "the oppressive character of gender rests not just on difference but the inferences from and the consequences of those differences." Applying West & Zimmerman's (1987, 2009) perspective to the small numbers of women in top management, gendered social systems that result from doing gender foster gender differences in candidates for top management positions that influence decisions to the disadvantage of female candidates.

Risman (2004, 2009) argued that West & Zimmerman's (1987) focus on doing gender was valuable but limited in its emphasis on an interactional level of analysis. In her view, gender represents a social structure equivalent in magnitude and impact to economics as a social structure; in other words, "Every society has a gender structure, in the same way that every society has an economic structure" (Risman, 2009, p. 83). Gender as a social structure has implications for phenomena at every level of analysis, not just the interactional level but also the individual, family, organizational, and societal levels. Applying Risman's (2004, 2009) perspective to the low numbers of women in top management, the structures within which organizational decision-makers attain positions of power and authority over who attains top management positions, as well as the institutionalized processes by which these decisions are made, are a consequence of gendered social systems to female candidates' disadvantage.

Acker (1990, 1998) offered a socialist feminist theory (Calás & Smircich, 1996) that focused explicitly on organizations as gendered institutions. She argued that organizations are not gender-neutral as commonly represented in the organization studies literature through the absence of any acknowledgment of gender. Instead, organizations represent combinations of divisions and categorizations, symbols and images, interactions, and logics within which the division of labor, the acceptability of some behaviors and not others, the assignment of power and authority, the assignment of physical space, the creation of part-time versus full-time jobs, and other structures and practices occur along gender lines. As a result, much of what transpires in organizations is a result of gendered processes that reflect the social systems in which work is organized and conducted. Applying Acker's (1990, 1998) perspective to the paucity of women in top management, women are disadvantaged by gendered organizational processes in most aspects of their jobs prior to their being in a position to be considered for top management, which in turn restricts whether they become candidates for and are selected for such positions.

Marxist feminist theories (e.g., Hartmann, 1976; Lorber, 1994) incorporate consideration of class relations as well as gender relations in social systems. Traditional Marxism has been characterized as blind to the gendered nature of social systems, including the shared ideological foundations of patriarchy (which it ignores) and capitalism (which it deplores: Greer & Greene, 2003; Hartmann, 1976). In contrast, according to Marxist feminist theorists, "Even though a hierarchy exists among men through a system of class, men as a group dominate and control women as a group, through a system of gender" (Calás & Smircich, 1996, p. 232). These structural arrangements divide work both in heterosexual households (in which women perform the majority of unpaid domestic work: Breen & Cooke, 2005; Warren, 2011) and in workplaces (in which men equivalent in class to women dominate positions of power and authority: Lorber, 1994). Thus, women are exploited both as unpaid and paid workers. Applying Marxist feminist theories (Hartmann, 1976; Lorber, 1994) to the low numbers of women in top management, candidates for such positions bring different experiences and receive differential treatment on the basis of socioeconomic class as well as gender.

Marxist feminist theories offer an intersectional perspective (Acker, 2006; Ridgeway & Kricheli-Katz, 2013; Rodriguez et al., 2016) by incorporating the influence of the intersection of gender and class on social systems. Other social-system-centered theories have extended an intersectional perspective by considering the intersection of gender, class, and race. For example, West & Fenstermaker's (1995) theory of "doing difference" focuses on the intersection of gender, class, and race as the basis for interactional processes in social systems that serve as the basis for social inequalities. In the same vein, Acker's (2006) theory of gender, class, and race in organizations focuses on how the intersection of these three social structures leads to "inequality regimes" in organizations that reflect inequalities at the societal level.

Social-system-centered theories that incorporate the intersection of gender and race have particular implications for the low numbers of women of color in top management. If women in general experience barriers to attaining top management positions, women of color experience even greater barriers (Parker & ogilvie, 1996; Rosette & Livingston, 2012; Rosette et al., 2016; Sanchez-Hucles & Davis, 2010); the barriers faced by women of color are discussed in detail in Chapter 4. As a result of a "concrete ceiling" (Piazza, 2016), women of color are the most underrepresented group in the top management ranks. Because of the preponderance of white men in top management positions, women of color are two degrees removed from what may be regarded as the white male top management prototype; in contrast, white women and men of color are one degree removed from this prototype. Intersectional social-system-centered theories that incorporate both race and gender (e.g., Acker, 2006; West & Fenstermaker, 1995) offer explanations for why there are especially small numbers of women of color in top management.

In summary, in this section of the chapter, I have briefly reviewed examples of person-centered, situation-centered, and social-system-centered theories, all of which offer explanations for why there are so few women in top management positions. There is an abundance of such theories, and a comprehensive review of all relevant theories is beyond the scope of this book. Next, I will revisit and review my personal research on the glass ceiling phenomenon conducted with Tony Butterfield, which yielded surprising results as well as implications for how glass ceilings may be shattered.

PERSONAL RESEARCH ON THE GLASS CEILING PHENOMENON

Tony and I were inspired in the late 1980s by the increased attention being devoted what was called the "glass ceiling." Since the term had been popularized in the media (Hymowitz & Schellhardt, 1986), it had taken on a life of its own and become prominent in scholarly discourse about the status of women in top management (e.g., Morrison & Von Glinow, 1990). However, no empirical field study had been conducted to date of the glass ceiling phenomenon. A fortuitous set of circumstances enabled us to fill this void in Powell & Butterfield (1994).

During a sabbatical leave, Tony held a job in the human resources office of a cabinet-level department of the US federal government. This office is responsible for keeping records of the decision-making process for all promotions in the department to and within the Senior Executive Service (SES), which consists of all nonmilitary top management positions in the US government except those reserved for political appointees; the top 1% of nonpolitical government positions are SES positions. By federal law, promotions to SES positions must be made systematically based on the same types of information across positions, and records of the decision process must be kept for at least two years. Tony's former boss was interested in exploring the notion of a glass ceiling within the federal government, which was conducting a study of glass ceilings in the corporate world of its own (US Department of Labor, 1991). In 1989, we were granted access to files, with identifying information removed, on the department's SES promotion decisions during the previous two years and were sent files for the next three years (i.e., from 1987 to 1992). Data from these files, copies of which arrived in several large cartons with identifying information blocked out by black magic marker (these were pre-Internet days), were coded and analyzed.

We tested two hypotheses with these data. In Hypothesis 1, invoking several existing situation-centered and social-system-centered theories described earlier, we proposed a direct effect of applicant gender on promotion decisions for top management positions favoring male candidates. In Hypothesis 2, we proposed indirect effects of applicant gender on promotion decisions through its relationships with human capital variables favoring male candidates. The rationale for Hypothesis 2 was as follows.

Stumpf and London (1981) identified criteria that are typically used in decisions about management promotions, including human capital variables such as relevant work experience, education, seniority, past performance, and being a current member of the promoting organization. Human capital theory (Becker, 1971) suggests that individuals make choices regarding investment in their human capital. Organizations also make choices regarding investments in their employees' human capital that may be subject to gender discrimination. If female applicants had accumulated less human capital over time than male applicants, their advancement to top management positions would be more restricted. Further, gender discrimination may have influenced evaluations of human capital, such that women were not given as much credit as men for the experience, education, and so on that they had accumulated. Female applicants whose human capital profiles were judged to be weaker than equivalent profiles of male applicants would be at a disadvantage, even if they were not directly discriminated against in promotion decisions to top management.

Powell & Butterfield (1994) describe the study methods. Briefly, when an SES position becomes open, a position announcement is circulated that specifies the criteria by which applicants will be judged. Interested individuals submit formal applications that provide background and career history data. The human resources office in the promoting department then screens out applicants that are considered obviously unqualified because they do not meet minimum eligibility criteria. The person who makes the final decision ("selecting official") typically is the future manager of the person to be selected for the position. The selecting official asks a panel of senior individuals who are familiar with the demands of the position to review the credentials of remaining applicants. The review panel evaluates each applicant on each of the specified criteria on a three-point scale. It also decides which applicants to "refer" to the selecting official, who then decides which of the referred applicants will be selected for the job.

Accordingly, we used three variables as measures of the outcomes of SES promotion decisions. The *review panel's evaluation* of the applicant's qualifications for the position was measured by the average of its ratings of the applicant on the specified criteria for the position. Whether the applicant was *referred* for the position by the review panel and, if referred, whether the applicant was *selected* for the position by the selecting official were the other two outcome measures. Overall, we received data on each of these outcome measures for 32 open SES positions that were filled within the department over a five-year period and for the 438 applicants, 88% of whom were male, who met minimum eligibility criteria for the position applied for. Six human capital variables were also measured for each applicant: whether the applicant was currently employed in the hiring department, the highest grade held in the federal government, years at the highest grade, years of full-time work experience, the highest degree obtained, and the most recent performance appraisal rating on a five-point scale.[1]

Complete results are presented in Powell and Butterfield (1994); here, I provide a brief summary. First, applicant gender had a significant effect on review panel evaluations. However, contrary to Hypothesis 1, the direction of the effect favored female applicants rather than male applicants. Further, contrary to Hypothesis 2, indirect effects of applicant gender on review panel evaluations through human capital variables also favored female applicants.

Second, applicant gender had a significant effect on referral decisions. However, contrary to Hypothesis 1 as for review panel evaluations, the direction of the effect favored female applicants rather than male applicants. Further, contrary to Hypothesis 2 as for review panel evaluations, indirect effects of gender on referral decisions through human capital variables also favored female applicants.

Finally, contrary to Hypothesis 1, applicant gender did not have a significant effect on selection decisions for the referred applicants. However, contrary to Hypothesis 2, indirect effects of gender through human capital variables on selection decisions favored female applicants over male applicants as for review panel evaluations and referral decisions.

You undoubtedly have noticed a pattern in these results. Our two hypotheses, that applicant gender would directly and indirectly influence promotion decisions for top management positions to the advantage of male applicants, were resoundingly rejected. Instead, all of the significant direct and indirect effects that were found favored female applicants. Tony and I were left with the challenge of how to interpret these unexpected findings. We did not view the results as refuting the existence of glass ceilings, as there was already a growing body of theory and evidence that glass ceilings operated to the disadvantage of women. Instead, we offered a situation-centered explanation for the results by considering the unique nature of the organization studied (Powell & Butterfield, 1994). The US federal government places a high degree of emphasis on procedural fairness (Greenberg, 1990) in making promotion decisions for SES positions. First, it requires that all open SES positions be posted publicly. Second, it requires that all SES promotion decisions be made using the same procedure. Third, it requires that records be kept of the entire decision-making process and retained for a two-year period. By providing structure to the decision-making process and enabling identification of decisions that are improperly made, these requirements put decision-makers on notice that they are accountable for their decision-making.

Further, the US government is particularly concerned with issues regarding equal employment opportunity. This concern was evident in its "glass ceiling initiative" (US Department of Labor, 1991) for private corporations as well as in established federal policies and practices. It may have led to women in the federal government benefitting more from promotion decisions for top management positions than in organizations with less of a concern for equal employment opportunity.

We also noted that the US government was highly unusual in granting researchers like us access to its promotion records. Tony and I could not imagine our approaching any business organization and receiving a favorable response to the question, "Would you be willing to give us access to your records for promotions to top management positions so we can analyze whether you have a glass ceiling?" Instead, we would be laughed out of the office if we ever got in. First, the existence of such records in corporate contexts seemed unlikely. As noted earlier, promotion decisions for top management positions tend to be based on subjective criteria (Antal & Krebsbach-Gnath, 1988) that are not easily codified. Second, the risks of corporate exposure about what these records might say would seem too high for them to be turned over to researchers for analysis; corporate lawyers would rule out that notion rather quickly.

Powell & Butterfield (1994) concluded that promotion decisions for top management positions that foster the glass ceiling phenomenon may be averted by organizational action, which in turn promotes organizational effectiveness and justice. Specifically, when procedures for promotion decisions to top management positions are standardized to increase the accountability of decision-makers and impose uniformity on the decision-making process, when these procedures are made known to all potential applicants, and when criteria for decisions are well established, qualified female candidates may fare at least as well as qualified male candidates. In contrast, when procedures are not standardized, or when criteria for promotion decisions are unspecified or vague, there is greater opportunity for gender discrimination favoring men to affect the outcomes of the promotion process.

CONCLUSIONS

Ever since Powell & Butterfield (1994) was published almost three decades ago, theories and explanations for the glass ceiling phenomenon have been extended and expanded considerably. However, although the study has been widely cited and reprinted in a collection of classic studies on women and management (Gatrell et al., 2010), its results and implications have been largely ignored.

Nonetheless, I stand by the study's implications for organizational effectiveness and justice as articulated in Powell & Butterfield (2015b). It identified specific practices that organizations may choose to adopt to minimize the existence of glass ceilings to women's disadvantage. I do not believe that women being advantaged rather than disadvantaged when promotions to top management positions are made, as Powell & Butterfield (1994) found, is desirable. In other words, I do not advocate that gender discrimination that favors women be substituted for gender discrimination that favors men in promotions to top management. Instead, I suggest that the most appropriate goal is for gender discrimination in such decisions to be minimized as much as possible, which would be facilitated by organizations adopting promotion procedures such as those described in Powell & Butterfield (1994).

In conclusion, I believe that we do not need more scholarly theories and explanations of glass ceilings. As this chapter has demonstrated, scholars already have many person-centered, situation-centered, and social-system-centered theories and explanations for the glass ceiling phenomenon to choose from. However, despite all of the scholarly attention glass ceilings have received over the last three decades, the nature of glass ceilings has remained essentially stable and there are still too few women in top management positions. Instead, we need more scholarly examination of practices that contribute to shattering glass ceilings (e.g., Powell & Butterfield, 1994) and widespread implementation of such practices in organizations.

Note

[1] In a later study of 300 applicants for SES positions for whom data on race were available (Powell & Butterfield, 1997), the small proportion and number of female applicants of color in the sample (3%, or nine applicants) rendered it inappropriate to reach a conclusion about the effect of the intersection of race and gender on promotion decision outcomes.

4

IS THERE A FEMALE ADVANTAGE OR DISADVANTAGE IN THE MANAGERIAL RANKS?

Pioneers of research on the linkage between gender and leadership (e.g., Bartol, 1978; Kanter, 1977; Marshall, 1984; Schein, 1973) probably never imagined that the question would arise as to whether there is a female advantage or disadvantage in the managerial ranks; indeed, as they were doggedly chronicling, conceptualizing, and studying female disadvantages, the prospect of anyone raising such a question would have shocked them at the time. However, according to a postfeminist sensibility at work (Gill et al., 2017) as described in Chapter 1, being a woman is an advantage, not a disadvantage. Are you convinced? Neither am I. Nonetheless, we need to explore the question because how it is answered is fundamental to understanding the linkage between gender and leadership.

The question may also seem surprising given the focus of earlier chapters of the book. Chapter 2 documented the continuing emphasis on masculinity, or traits generally associated with males, in leader stereotypes. Although there has been a gradual decline in this emphasis, it seems unlikely to disappear in the foreseeable future or shift to an emphasis on femininity such that what is now a female disadvantage is converted into a female advantage. In the same vein, Chapter 3 documented the continuing few number of women in top management. Despite an ever-so-gradual increase in female membership, the executive ranks of corporations remain overwhelmingly male-dominated, and trends in their composition hardly signal a female advantage to come. Chapters 2 and 3 clearly chronicle female disadvantages in the managerial ranks, not female advantages.

Women also experience disadvantages in the managerial ranks that go beyond the negative consequences of leader stereotypes and the glass ceiling phenomenon documented in earlier chapters. A self-reinforcing cycle of women's illegitimacy as leaders promotes a backlash towards their occupying leader roles that may reduce their effectiveness once in these roles due to negative subordinate behaviors and reduced cooperation (Rudman & Glick, 2001; Vial et al., 2016). As a result, female leaders as a group may be subjected to outright prejudice due to their very presence in the leader role (Eagly & Karau, 2002) that puts them at a distinct disadvantage compared with male leaders as a group.

Further, there are female disadvantages in society in general that go beyond any disadvantages incurred due to the linkage between gender and leadership. For example, women as a group are subjected to sexism, or prejudice on the basis of gender (Glick & Rudman, 2010), to a far greater extent than men as a group (Glick & Fiske, 1999). When racism, or prejudice on the basis of race/ethnicity (Dovidio et al., 2010), is combined with sexism, women of color as a group (as they are often labeled, although the term "of color" includes many different subgroups on the basis of race/ethnicity) are subjected to what may be called "gendered racism" (Lewis et al., 2017) compared with men of color or white women. Further, according to social-system-centered theories invoked in Chapter 3 (e.g., Acker, 1990; Lorber, 1994; Risman, 2004; West & Zimmerman, 1987), women are disadvantaged in virtually all of their societal roles, not just the leader or top executive role; social-system-centered theories that address the intersection of gender and race (e.g., Acker, 2006; West & Fenstermaker, 2005) suggest that women of color especially experience societal disadvantages.

Nonetheless, a vigorous debate over the question of whether there is a female advantage in the managerial ranks rather than a female disadvantage has emerged in recent years (e.g., Eagly & Carli, 2003; Eagly et al., 2014; Vecchio, 2002), albeit for very different reasons. Person-centered, situation-centered, and social-system-centered theories and explanations have been offered for the existence of a female advantage. For example, a person-centered explanation that has received considerable media (e.g., "Room for debate," 2009; Sharpe, 2000) and scholarly (e.g., Eagly et al., 2003) attention suggests that female leaders are simply superior to male leaders, thereby giving women a natural advantage in leader roles in general. A situation-centered explanation suggests that the extent to which such a female advantage is manifested, if at all, is influenced by the nature of the organizational context in which leadership occurs, thereby suggesting a moderating role of situational factors (e.g., Eagly et al., 1995). A social-system-centered explanation suggests that equal employment opportunity (EEO) laws in many nations (Archibong & Sharps, 2013; Crosby et al., 2006; Davies & Robison, 2016; Myors et al., 2008) institute a female advantage that would not otherwise exist; further, this explanation suggests that women of color experience a "double advantage" on the basis of gender and race rather than a "double whammy" (Bell et al., 1993).

In this chapter, I consider arguments and support for a female advantage versus a female disadvantage in the managerial ranks. Selected aspects of the linkage between gender and leadership are reviewed that may promote a female advantage or disadvantage beyond those already considered in Chapters 2 and 3. The double advantage versus double whammy debate over the experiences of women of color in the managerial ranks and an intersectional perspective of these experiences is given particular attention. Finally, I offer conclusions based on this review that address the question in the chapter title.

IF YOU HAD A CHOICE …

One way of discovering individuals' preferences for female versus male leaders, which may confer a female advantage or disadvantage, is to conduct polls. These preferences may reflect personal biases or experiences and influence responses to actual leaders. Since the 1950s, the Gallup Organization has regularly asked random samples of adults in various countries (e.g., the United Kingdom, the United States, Canada, Spain, Iceland) the same question: "If you were taking a new job and had your choice of a boss, would you prefer to work for a man or a woman?" (e.g., Carroll, 2006; Simmons, 2001); respondents could also state that the gender of their new boss would make no difference to them. Historically, all over the globe, people who stated a preference have tended to prefer a male boss over a female boss (Simmons, 2001); in no country has a preference for a female boss over a male boss been expressed. These poll results support the existence of a female disadvantage in the managerial ranks.

However, according to the most recent Gallup poll results, which were obtained from an American sample (Brenan, 2017), this tendency may be in decline. A majority of adults (55%) stated that the gender of their boss would make no difference to them, and roughly equal percentages stated that they would prefer a male boss (23%) or a female boss (21%).

In these results, leader preferences differed according to the age of the person being asked (Brenan, 2017). Overall, American adults younger than 35 preferred a female boss over a male boss when they expressed a preference. Younger respondents may have been more likely to prefer a female boss than older respondents because they had greater experience in working with women as peers in educational programs and jobs. These results suggest that a generational shift may be taking place in leader preferences towards a greater preference for female leaders. If leader preferences for younger respondents in the Gallup results are mirrored in future generations, a bias favoring female leaders could replace the bias that once favored male leaders as new entrants to the labor force progress in their careers, which would lead to an eventual female advantage in the managerial ranks.

Leader preferences also differed according to the intersection of respondents' gender and age (Brenan, 2017). Women under age 50 preferred a female boss over a male boss, whereas women 50 and older were more divided. In contrast, men 50 and older preferred a male boss over a female boss, whereas men under age 50 were more divided. The finding that younger women and older men had more clear-cut leader preferences than older women and younger men respectively is interesting. It suggests the potential for a clash between individuals over the linkage between gender and leadership on the basis of the intersection of their gender and age.

Further, leader preferences differed according to the intersection of employed respondents' gender and their current boss's gender (Brenan, 2017). About one-third of employed respondents stated that they have a female boss. Those with a female boss preferred a female boss over a male boss, whereas those with a male boss preferred a male boss over a female boss. Due to the increased presence of women in management (Powell, 2019), more employees than ever before have had a female boss. In fact, many employees have become accustomed to working for a woman, having had two or more female bosses in their careers.

This trend in itself may have contributed to the shift in leader preferences over time. In studies of actual managers and their subordinates (Bhatnagar & Swamy, 1995; Ezell et al., 1981), subordinates did not respond differently to male and female managers for whom they have actually worked. The experience of having been supervised by a woman contributes to more positive attitudes toward women as leaders. Being in direct contact with or proximity to women as leaders may serve to dispel biases against women holding leader roles. However, individuals' attitudes toward women as leaders do not become more positive with experience unless that experience itself is positive.

Individuals' leader preferences may also be influenced by their gender identity, or beliefs about the extent to which they possess psychological traits associated with gender stereotypes (Bem, 1974). Tony Butterfield and I (2015c) asked survey respondents to answer the exact same Gallup poll question and also to describe themselves on the independent masculinity and femininity scales of the Short Bem Sex-Role Inventory (Bem, 1981). When they expressed a preference, respondents who described themselves as highly masculine were more likely to prefer a male boss, whereas those who described themselves as highly feminine were more likely to prefer a female boss. In contrast, respondents who described themselves as possessing similar levels of masculine and feminine traits were less likely to express any preference for a male or female boss (Powell & Butterfield, 2015c).

In summary, although there has been an overall tendency to prefer a male boss over a female boss, recent evidence suggests that this tendency may be diminishing or disappearing. Poll and research results suggest that the preference to work for a male or female leader may be influenced by respondents' gender, gender identity, age, and the gender of their current boss in ways that confer a female advantage or disadvantage in the managerial ranks.

DO WOMEN MAKE BETTER BOSSES?

Ever since the proportion of female managers began to rise starting in the 1970s in virtually all countries (Powell & Graves, 2003), considerable media and scholarly attention have been devoted to the question of whether women or men, if either, make better bosses. Questions about gender differences among managers stimulate especially heated debate. This is because corporate leaders are given an enormous amount of attention, especially in societies that place a high value on individualism rather than collectivism such as the United States, Australia, the United Kingdom, Canada, the Netherlands, and New Zealand (Hofstede, 2001). In highly individualistic societies, the success of organizations is attributed to the wisdom, values, and practices of their founders or current leaders. When organizations fail to achieve expected results, their leaders are the first to be blamed. Consider the issues of gender (which has always been a topic of keen public interest) and leadership together and it is clear why so many people from all walks of life have strong opinions about what constitutes effective leadership as well as who is more likely to exhibit it.

In this section, I address first the attention given to this question in the popular media, drawing on my personal experiences, and then review theories and research on the question.

My 15 minutes of media fame

As an example of the enormous amount of public interest in this question, I would like to describe my own 15 minutes of fame (or notoriety, depending on your perspective) in discussing it about a decade ago. The *New York Times* had recently published an interview with Carol Smith, a media executive, about her views on leadership (Bryant, 2009). In the interview, Ms Smith said, "In my experience, female bosses tend to be better managers, better advisors, mentors, rational thinkers. Men love to hear themselves talk." She added that she intentionally arrives late for meetings with men to miss their inevitably boring conversations about sports events and teams before the meeting actually starts. Sharpe (2000, p. 75), in a special report in a popular business magazine, expressed a similar sentiment in support of a female leadership advantage: "As leaders, women rule."

After the interview triggered an outpouring of comments and media attention, the *Times* invited six people to participate in an online debate one week later over the question, "Do women make better bosses?" ("Room for debate," 2009). I was one of the participants in this debate; the other five participants, all women, included Alice Eagly (a great scholar whose research I have frequently cited in this book) as well as consultants and executives. In my contribution to the debate (Powell, 2009), I briefly summarized some of the research described later in this chapter as well as research on the linkage between leader and gender stereotypes described in Chapter 2. Nothing controversial, or so I thought.

After readers were invited to post comments on the online debate, over 500 responses were received. Several themes emerged in the responses. One theme was criticism of the composition of the debate panel itself. The panel was alternatively disparaged as "five females and one guy who wants to make his wife happy" (not knowing that my wife, Laura Graves, is a prolific scholar who has frequently been my co-author as well), "five women and one man who was formerly the Chair of the Women in Management Division of the Academy of Management" (implying that this credential provided a good basis to dismiss anything I had to say), and "five women and one boomer man" (an assessment made presumably after seeing my web page photo). Thus the female-dominated panel, with me seen as the token male who was likely to be biased due to my very presence on the panel, obviously troubled some readers.

Many respondents took strong positions on the question that was posed, writing passionately about their experiences pro and con with female bosses, male bosses, or both. From these experiences, they tended to draw conclusions about what *all* male bosses and *all* female bosses are like, a tendency that was encouraged by the nature of the question being debated.

Some respondents answered "yes" to the question and argued that women are better bosses. For example, "In my experience, women make better bosses. Generally, they do not have that asinine alpha male schoolyard crap baggage." "There is a clear advantage: You won't be bombarded with noxious sports analogies (echoing Carol Smith's comments)." "The one female boss I have had is the best boss of my life."

Other respondents answered "no" to the question and argued that men are better bosses. For example, "I can't understand them, so how can I work for them?" "My experience found [women] to be excellent employees, but terrible managers as if they were trying to prove themselves as equals more than anything." "As a female, I'll take the male egos any day. At least you know what to expect from a guy. Men are more level tempered. They lay it on the line. Women are egotistical bit__es."

A few respondents argued that neither women nor men make better bosses. For example, "Women are no better or worse than men, in general. There are only good managers and bad managers." "I have had good and bad experiences with both sexes. It completely depends upon the individual and not the sex."

Still other respondents argued that both male and female bosses leave a lot to be desired. For example, "I have had two female bosses. Both were dishonest and manipulative. The male bosses I had were merely incompetent."

Here is my favorite response of all: "All bosses suck. This is a trick question."

As the online debate continued to rage in the comments section, it turned on itself as some women criticized what they perceived as a sexist tone exhibited in many of the previous comments from men. For example, "The outpouring of 'women make the most inferior, back-stabbing, emotional, menopausal, passive-aggressive, ineffectual, lazy bosses' or 'have a family' sentiment in these comments is a pretty stark picture of how overt sexism is still alive and acceptable today." "This [dealing with men who say, such as in an earlier comment, 'I can't understand them, so how can I work for them?'] is one of the challenges women have faced in working for/with men. We deal with it. I suggest you do the same." "The vitriol with which so many male commenters have greeted this [debate] demonstrates well the obstacles that women still face in the workplace."

As I said earlier, this is a heated topic! Although the media episode in which I played a role occurred about a decade ago, the question of whether women or men, if either, make better bosses has never gone away, at least in the popular media. If you doubt this point, try searching Google on the question, "Do women make better bosses?" At the time of writing, I found about 56 million entries in my own Google search.

Theories and research

Meanwhile, scholars have been weighing in on the same question since the 1970s, with a considerable body of research having accumulated over time (Broadbridge & Hearn, 2008; Broadbridge & Simpson, 2011). Gender similarities and differences have been examined in a wide array of personal characteristics of managers, including their personalities, motivation, commitment, values, self-confidence, stress, and behaviors or leadership style (cf. Marshall, 1984; Powell, 1988). A full review of the literature on the linkages between managers' gender and personal characteristics is beyond the scope of this book. So, in this section of the chapter, I focus on the linkage between gender and leadership style, and in turn the linkage between leadership style and effectiveness, because the questions of which leadership styles are most associated with leader effectiveness and who is most likely to exhibit these leadership styles get to the heart of the issues raised in the online debate.

Further, in the leadership literature, many different types of leadership styles have been conceptualized and examined, including but not limited to the initiating structure and consideration dimensions of leadership (Bartol & Butterfield, 1976), autocratic versus democratic leadership (Eagly & Johnson, 1990), authentic leadership (Gardner et al., 2011), servant leadership (Parris & Peachey, 2013), and transformational and transactional leadership (Bass, 1985, 1998; Díaz-Sáenz, 2011). Because transformational and transactional leadership have received the most attention in leadership theories and research in recent decades (Díaz-Sáenz, 2011; Powell et al., 2008), I focus on the linkages among transformational and transactional leadership (along with laissez-faire leadership, as explained below), gender, and leader effectiveness in this chapter.

Bass (1985, 1998) argued that leaders may be both transformational and transactional. Transformational leadership motivates subordinates to transcend their own self-interests for the good of the group or organization by setting exceptionally high standards for performance and then developing subordinates to achieve these standards. Although definitions of these leadership styles have been adapted over time, transformational leaders are regarded to exhibit four types of behavior: (1) *charisma* or idealized influence, by displaying attributes that induce subordinates to view them as role models and behaviors that communicate a sense of values, purpose, and the importance of the mission; (2) *inspirational motivation*, by exuding optimism and excitement about the mission and its attainability; (3) *intellectual stimulation*, by encouraging subordinates to question basic assumptions and consider problems and tasks from new perspectives; and (4) *individualized consideration*, by focusing on the development and mentoring of subordinates as individuals and attending to their specific needs (Bass, 1985, 1998; Eagly et al., 2003).

Transactional leadership focuses on clarifying the responsibilities of subordinates and then responding to how well subordinates execute those responsibilities. Transactional leaders exhibit two kinds of behavior: (a) *contingent reward*, by promising and providing suitable rewards if subordinates achieve their assigned objectives; and (b) *management by exception*, by intervening to correct subordinate performance either in anticipation of a problem or after a problem has occurred. Leaders who engage in active management by exception systematically monitor subordinate performance for mistakes, whereas those who engage in passive management by exception wait for subordinate difficulties to be brought to their attention before intervening (Bass, 1985, 1998; Eagly et al., 2003).

In contrast to transformational and transactional leadership, laissez-faire leadership, which is often examined in conjunction with these two leadership styles, is regarded as a general absence of leadership. Laissez-faire leaders avoid taking responsibility for leadership altogether by refraining from giving direction, making decisions, or involving themselves in the development of their subordinates (Eagly et al., 2003).

Before we examine gender differences in actual leadership styles, let's consider the ways in which gender considerations may influence behavior in leader roles. Transformational leadership is positively associated with nurturance and agreeableness, feminine or communal traits in gender stereotypes (Ellemers, 2018; Kite et al., 2008), and negatively associated with aggressiveness, a masculine or agentic trait in gender stereotypes (Ross & Offermann, 1997). Individualized consideration is congruent with the feminine gender stereotype because its developmental focus reflects a high concern with relationships and the needs of others. However, both active and passive management by exception are congruent with the masculine gender stereotype in their focus on correcting followers' mistakes because they stress immediate task accomplishment over long-term building of relationships and favor the use of the leadership position to dominate others. In addition, contingent reward is congruent with the masculine gender stereotype because it is task-oriented rather than interpersonal-oriented. Laissez-faire leadership is not associated with either the masculine or feminine gender stereotype. Overall, transformational leadership appears to be more congruent with the feminine than the masculine gender stereotype, whereas transactional leadership appears to be more congruent with the masculine than the feminine gender stereotype (Bass et al., 1996; Kark, 2004).

According to social role theory (Eagly, 1987; Eagly & Wood, 2012), male and female leaders hold positions in organizational hierarchies that are defined both by the demands of the position and the constraints of their gender role. Although leader roles with the same demands would seem to call for the same behaviors, female leaders' behaviors may differ from those of male leaders because they face unique gender constraints. As discussed in Chapter 2, female leaders face the challenge of dealing with the perceived incongruity between the leader role and their assigned gender role (Eagly & Karau, 2002), whereas male leaders face no such challenge. In response to this perceived incongruity, female leaders may embrace the transformational leadership style more than men because its communal qualities being cast in a positive light enhances their legitimacy as leaders (Eagly et al., 2003). Moreover, because women are held to a higher standard than men in attaining leader roles, they may need to display a transformational leadership style to a greater extent than men to meet the higher standard.

Eagly et al. (2003) explored these issues in a meta-analysis of gender differences in transformational, transactional, and laissez-faire leadership. They found that actual female leaders are more transformational than their male counterparts (Eagly et al., 2003). Women were rated higher than men on all dimensions of transformational leadership: charisma (especially attributes that motivate pride and respect), inspirational motivation, intellectual stimulation, and individualized consideration. Women also were rated higher than men on the contingent reward dimension of transactional leadership. In contrast, men were rated higher than women on the active and passive management by exception dimensions of transactional leadership and in laissez-faire leadership.

Several meta-analyses have been conducted of the linkages of transformational and transactional leadership to leader effectiveness (Judge & Piccolo, 2004; Lowe et al., 1996; Wang et al., 2011). Overall, these meta-analyses suggest that all of the dimensions of transformational leadership and the contingent reward dimension of transactional leadership are positively associated with leader effectiveness as reflected in individual, group, and organizational performance. In contrast, the passive management by exception dimension of transactional leadership and the laissez-faire leadership are negatively associated with leader effectiveness.

Cumulatively, what do these various meta-analyses tell us? If we combine meta-analytic results of the linkages of gender to transformational and transactional leadership with meta-analytic results of the linkages of transformational and transactional leadership to leader effectiveness, we find that (1) women are rated higher than men in behaviors that contribute to their effectiveness as leaders, and (2) women are rated lower than men in behaviors that detract from their effectiveness as leaders. In short, these meta-analyses suggest a person-centered explanation for a female advantage in the managerial ranks, specifically that women make better bosses in terms of leadership style than men. This explanation is consistent with claims in the popular media (e.g., Bryant, 2009; Sharpe, 2000) that women have superior leadership skills.

However, situational factors may influence the extent to which this female advantage is manifested. For example, male leaders may be more effective than female leaders in male-intensive settings (e.g., the military), whereas female leaders may be more effective than male leaders in female-intensive settings (e.g., education, social services; Eagly et al., 1995). Male leaders may be more effective than female leaders when the particular leader role examined is more congruent with the male gender role, whereas female leaders may be more effective than male leaders when the particular leader role examined is more congruent with the female gender role. Further, male leaders may be more effective than female leaders in lower-level management positions, whereas female leaders may be more effective than male leaders in middle-level management positions (Eagly et al., 1995). The position of middle manager is often regarded as requiring heavy use of interpersonal skills to wield influence, which would favor women according to gender stereotypes. Thus, a situation-centered explanation suggests that characteristics of the organizational context influence the presence of a female advantage or disadvantage in the managerial ranks, or the absence of any gender-based advantage.

An intriguing meta-analysis focused on the source of perceptions of leader effectiveness (Paustian-Underdahl et al., 2014). When self-ratings of leader effectiveness were examined, men rated themselves as more effective leaders than women rated themselves. In contrast, when others' ratings of leader effectiveness (e.g., ratings by bosses, subordinates, or peers) were examined, women were rated as more effective leaders than men. These results suggest that men overestimate and women underestimate their own leader effectiveness compared with how others perceive them as leaders. That is, in men's views, there is a male advantage in leader effectiveness that is not supported by observers' perceptions of a female advantage. Here is an example of what overconfidence in your own leadership abilities, which men have been found to possess as a group in abundance (Reuben et al., 2012), may get you: glory in your own mind (i.e., "What a great leader I am!"), if not in the eyes of others.

In conclusion, results of meta-analyses, which synthesize evidence across research studies, suggest a female leadership advantage. However, situational factors are likely to influence whether this advantage is displayed in a given organizational context. Also, as the results regarding leader preferences reported earlier in this chapter suggest, as well as the media debate over whether women make better bosses, who possesses an advantage in the managerial ranks, if anyone, may depend on who you ask.

DO EQUAL EMPLOYMENT OPPORTUNITY LAWS GRANT ADVANTAGES ON THE BASIS OF GENDER AND RACE?

Many nations have passed some form of EEO legislation (Archibong & Sharps, 2013; Crosby et al., 2006; Davies & Robison, 2016; Konrad & Linnehan, 1999). Examples of EEO laws include the United Kingdom's Equality Act 2010, the United States' Title VII of the Civil Rights Act and Equal Pay Act, Canada's Employment Equity Act, Australia's Sex Discrimination Act, Japan's Equal Employment Opportunity Law, the Netherlands' Equal Pay and Equal Treatment Acts, and Denmark's Equal Treatment and Anti-Discrimination Acts (Myors et al., 2008); the European Union's Employment Equality Framework Directive provides guidance for the EEO laws of its member nations. Although the details of these laws and the groups that are targeted by the laws vary by nation, virtually all EEO laws share the objectives of banning discrimination in employment practices on the basis of gender and race.

In addition to banning discrimination, EEO laws often specify what kinds of actions organizations may take or are required to take to overcome the effects of past discrimination and allow members of a protected group to compete on equal terms with members of the favored group. Legally mandated or permitted policies and practices for this purpose have alternatively been referred to by terms such as "positive action" in the United Kingdom (Davies & Robison, 2016), "affirmative action" in the United States (Harrison et al., 2006), "employment equity" in Canada (Hideg et al., 2011), and other terms in different nations.

Laws and courts in various nations have ruled on what kinds of organizational policies and practices are legal and what are illegal. For example, in the United Kingdom, positive action is legal as long as the employer meets the conditions of relevant EEO laws. Examples of positive action would be implementing a mentoring program for female managers to improve their prospects for advancement, or launching a recruitment campaign to increase the proportion of members of racial or ethnic minority groups in the applicant pool for a managerial job (Noon, 2010). Positive actions seek to redress past disadvantages experienced by members of protected groups, but they do not take these disadvantages specifically into account when making decisions about matters such as selection and promotion. However, what has been called "positive discrimination" is generally illegal. Examples of positive discrimination would be hiring candidates for managerial jobs only because of their protected group membership (e.g., gender or racial/ethnic group) rather than being the most qualified candidates, or setting quotas to hire a specific number of candidates from a particular protected group[1] (Noon, 2010; XpertHR, 2020). In the United States, the same kind of distinction between legal and illegal affirmative action policies has been generally upheld in the courts (Konrad & Linnehan, 1999; Sedmak & Vidas, 1994).

Organizations differ in their EEO cultures regardless of mandates about what constitutes legal versus illegal practices. Some organizations are proactive in setting and pursuing EEO goals, other organizations are reactive in seeking to achieve minimal compliance with EEO laws, and still other organizations ignore EEO laws in the hope that they will not be enforced (Pati, 1977; Powell, 1993). When the organizational culture places a strong emphasis on EEO, whether for proactive or reactive reasons, decision-makers are rewarded according to their achievement of EEO goals and may seek to maximize their rewards by favoring members of protected groups (e.g., women and people of color) in their personnel decisions. In contrast, when the organizational culture does not promote EEO or avoids the mandates of EEO laws, decision-makers are freer to act on their personal inclinations, which may incorporate biases that operate to the disadvantage of protected group members.

Legal mandates about EEO are often poorly understood (Crosby et al., 2006). For example, people who fail to understand the distinction between positive action and positive discrimination tend to react negatively to the former when their primary objection is to the latter (Noon, 2010). They may believe that positive action or affirmative action practices inevitably involve quotas, when such practices actually vary widely and typically do not involve quotas (Crosby et al., 2006; Powell, 2019).

Legal mandates about EEO are also controversial, and there are strong differences in attitudes towards them on the basis of personal characteristics. A meta-analysis of attitudes toward affirmative action in the US found that women had more positive attitudes than men, and that both African Americans and Hispanic Americans had more positive attitudes than white Americans (Harrison et al., 2006). These results are consistent with the norm of self-interest that underlies many theories of human behavior (Miller, 1999) because women and people of color are typically classified as protected groups by EEO laws. Also consistent with the norm of self-interest, white men are least supportive of affirmative action and most likely to view it as constituting "reverse discrimination" (Coston & Kimmel, 2013).

Also in Harrison and colleagues' (2006) meta-analysis, highly sexist and highly racist individuals had more negative attitudes toward affirmative action and were inclined to view it as granting unfair advantages to women and people of color respectively. Because affirmative action is intended to help the very people who tend to be rejected by sexists and racists, these negative attitudes are consistent with theories of prejudice on the basis of gender (Glick & Rudman, 2010) and race (Dovidio et al., 2010).

In summary, EEO laws are intended to ban future discrimination and remedy past discrimination on the basis of gender, race, and other personal characteristics depending on the nation. Whether they actually grant advantages on the basis of gender and race depends in part on the emphasis of organizational EEO cultures. Further, similar to preferences for a male versus female boss and beliefs about whether women make better bosses, whether EEO laws are perceived as granting advantages on the basis of gender and race depends on who you ask.

DOUBLE ADVANTAGE, DOUBLE WHAMMY, OR SOMETHING MORE COMPLEX?

The previous section focused on the impact of EEO laws on the experiences of women and people of color considered separately. But what about the experiences of women of color? Different perspectives have been offered on the nature of these experiences.

One perspective is that women of color experience a double advantage in the managerial ranks if organizational cultures that promote EEO propel them ahead of members of other groups to count as a "double minority" (Bell et al., 1993). Nkomo (1988, p. 136) labeled this notion a "two-fer theory," with a woman of color assigned one point because she is a person of color and a second point because she is female when corporations attempt to meet their EEO goals, thereby granting them a privileged status over men of color and white women as well as white men.

Other arguments have been advanced for women of color having a double advantage. For example, based on a study of black managerial and professional women, Epstein (1973) argued that three differential patterns accounted for their career success. First, possessing one group membership (e.g., being female) that conferred a disadvantage cancelled out the negative effect of the other group membership (e.g., being a person of color), thereby neutralizing any disadvantages that might result from their multiple group memberships. Second, these two group memberships combined to grant women of color a positive status in professions that enhanced rather than reduced their bargaining power. Third, women of color were insulated from cultural diversions by their unique status, thereby strengthening their career motivation and ambition (Epstein, 1973).

An opposing perspective is that women of color are victims of a "double whammy" and have lower status in the managerial ranks than either white women or men of color (Bell et al., 1993). Although sexism and racism are parallel processes that differ in some respects (Reid, 1988), women of color are subjected to both types of prejudice simultaneously, thereby making it especially difficult for them to enter and advance in the managerial ranks (Davidson, 1997).

Other arguments have been advanced for women of color experiencing a double whammy. For example, as noted earlier in the book, female candidates offer a lesser fit for leader positions to be filled than male candidates according to gender-based prototypes for leader roles (Perry et al., 1994), thereby putting them at a disadvantage; applying the same argument, leader prototypes based on both gender and race may put women of color at a double disadvantage. In support of this notion, Rosette and Livingston (2012) found that black female executives were evaluated more negatively and disproportionally sanctioned under conditions of poor organizational performance than black male, white female, or white male executives. These results suggest that black women experience a double whammy in leader roles: "Because the schematic representation of a typical leader does not encompass Blacks when race is considered or women when gender is considered, Black women may be disadvantaged relative to other groups that share a greater degree of schematic overlap" (Rosette & Livingston, 2012, p. 1162).

However, the double advantage versus double whammy debate over the nature of the experiences of women of color in the managerial ranks seems too simplistic. For example, the arguments for a double advantage stemming from EEO laws assume that the positive effects of these laws for women of color are additive on the basis of gender and race. In the same vein, the arguments for a double disadvantage stemming from the combined effects of sexism and racism or a lack of fit with leader prototypes assume that the negative effects of these processes for women of color are additive on the basis of gender and race. What is missing from this debate is the notion of intersectionality (Acker, 2006; Ridgeway & Kricheli-Katz, 2013; Rodriguez et al., 2016; Rosette et al., 2018; Smooth, 2010). That is, the intersection of gender and race may result in women of color having more complex experiences when seeking to enter or advance in the managerial ranks than either a double-advantage or double-whammy perspective would suggest.

For example, women of color may adopt a leadership style that reflects the intersection of their group memberships. Parker and ogilvie (1996) suggested that black female leaders, consistent with stereotypes of black women in general, may possess traits that are associated with both the masculine gender stereotype (e.g., self-confidence, autonomy, independence) and the feminine gender stereotype (e.g., supportive, considerate, sensitive to the needs of others). Overall, the intersection of gender and race may contribute to the differential shaping of leadership styles of women from various non-white cultures (Eagly & Chin, 2010).

As another example of an intersectional perspective, Smith et al. (2019) found that Black female executives experience what may be called "intersectional invisibility." That is, because of their belonging to intersecting groups on the basis of gender and race, they are both invisible (few in number, likely to be overlooked) and hypervisible (standing out among their executive peers, likely to be highly scrutinized). The combination of invisibility and hypervisibility confers "outsider within" status to black female executives, which in turn contributes to their experiencing either benign intersectional invisibility, in which case the effects of their gender and race cancel each other (Epstein, 1973), or hostile intersectional invisibility, in which case the negative effects of their gender and race strengthen each other (Smith et al., 2019). Thus, the intersection of Black female executives' gender and race may yield no overall effect or a double disadvantage depending on the direction of the intersectional effect. The results of this study are more complex than competing double advantage versus double whammy hypotheses suggest.

In summary, the experiences of women of color in the managerial ranks may be characterized by a double advantage, double whammy, or intersectional perspective. An intersectional perspective seems especially promising in shedding light on the unique experiences of women of color in the managerial ranks.

CONCLUSIONS

Is there a female advantage or disadvantage in the managerial ranks? This chapter's review of selected aspects of the linkage between gender and leadership that may promote a female advantage or disadvantage, combined with other aspects reviewed in Chapters 2 and 3, make it clear that there is no clear-cut answer to this question. Rather than "a female advantage" or "a female disadvantage," the best answer to the question suggested by scholarly theories and research may be "both." Another answer to this question, if we consider strongly held feelings about it in the general public, is, "It depends on who you ask."

Supporting a female advantage, women as a group have been found in meta-analyses to display a leadership style that renders them more effective leaders than men as a group. Also, the combination of EEO laws and organizational cultures that emphasize compliance with these laws may grant women an advantage, but only if actions taken in compliance go beyond overcoming the effects of a past female disadvantage and confer an overall female advantage.

Supporting a female disadvantage, people have tended to prefer a male boss over a female boss if they had a choice, but this tendency may be diminishing over time and its presence or absence depends on who you ask. Sexism also contributes to a female disadvantage. Further, the linkage between leader and gender stereotypes documented in Chapter 2, as well as gendered organizational and societal processes suggested by situation-centered and social-system-centered theories documented in Chapter 3, contribute to a female disadvantage.

Thus, we do not need to choose between the two alternative views posed in the chapter's title. Instead, both views may hold. Women may be advantaged in the leadership styles they tend to adopt when given the chance, but they may also be disadvantaged in gaining access to the managerial ranks of organizations to get the chance and advancing within these ranks.

Whether these competing processes are equal in strength and offset each other, thereby resulting in no net female advantage or disadvantage in the managerial ranks, or are unequal in strength and result in an overall female advantage or disadvantage, is a question this review cannot answer. Extant theories and research provide inconsistent guidance, and most studies are too narrowly defined to address the question in a comprehensive manner.

In the same vein, scholars have considered whether women of color experience a double advantage or double whammy in the managerial ranks. However, we do not need to choose between these two options either.

Instead, an intersectional approach to theory and research that incorporates the interaction between gender and race seems the most promising way to advance our understanding of women of color's managerial experiences.

In conclusion, the question in the chapter title is a source of contention among scholars as well as in the popular media (as I have learned from experience). I anticipate that it will continue to be a subject of debate whenever the topic of gender and leadership is discussed for the foreseeable future.

Note

[1] It should be noted that gender quotas for corporate boards of directors, which are governing bodies that oversee organizations in the interests of shareholders, have been legally mandated in several countries (Hughes et al., 2017). This is a rare instance in which quotas on the basis of gender have been incorporated into law.

5

WHY DO (SOME) MEN IN TOP MANAGEMENT FEEL FREE TO SEXUALLY HARASS WOMEN?

On October 5, 2017, allegations that Harvey Weinstein, co-founder and then CEO of the Weinstein Company (a prominent movie studio) had engaged in truly despicable behavior towards women – quid pro quo sexual harassment, sexual assault, and rape over a period of almost three decades – became public knowledge (Kantor & Twohey, 2017). This pattern of behavior had persisted despite prior internal circulation of a memo detailing sexual harassment and other misconduct by Weinstein; many board members and company executives were already aware of Weinstein's behavior towards women. On many occasions, he had reached financial settlements with women he had harassed that included nondisclosure agreements, which legally prevented them from speaking out about his behavior. It took public exposure of his appalling behavior to force the company's all-male board of directors to act. Three days after the initial allegations were published, Weinstein was fired by the remaining board members, one-third of whom had already resigned upon learning of the allegations or seeing the allegations go public. Within months, the company had filed for bankruptcy (Kantor & Twohey, 2019).

It seemed like a dam broke with the Weinstein allegations. A flood of further allegations against Weinstein from over 90 women (Ransom, 2020) as well as allegations against other powerful men soon followed (Gill & Orgad, 2018; Mendes et al., 2018; Peters & Besley, 2019). A hashtag movement called "#MeToo," based on the original Me Too movement that was founded before hashtags even existed (Onwuachi-Willig, 2018), was launched by victims of sexual harassment in support of other victims, with hundreds of thousands of women sharing their experiences (Ransom, 2020). Sexual harassment in the workplace, a topic that has received scholarly attention since the 1970s (e.g., Gutek, 1985; MacKinnon, 1979; O'Leary-Kelly et al., 2009), once again became a focus of considerable media attention. How sexual harassment was viewed by the public seemed qualitatively different than in the past, with deeper and more sustained outrage than earlier allegations of sexual harassment by powerful men had triggered.

However, if the Weinstein allegations were unique, it was only in the level of depravity at top management levels that they portrayed. Numerous reports of rampant sexual harassment by other powerful men came to light in the wake of the #MeToo movement. In the year after the Weinstein allegations became public knowledge, the movement was reported to have brought down 201 powerful men and three powerful women, including the heads of Amazon Studios, Barnes & Noble, Wynn Resorts, and the CBS Corporation (Carlsen et al., 2018).

In some cases, organized actions by employees triggered corporate actions against sexual harassment in high places. For example, after the global technology company Google asked for the resignation of a top executive due to a sexual harassment complaint that it judged to be credible, it softened the blow by giving him a $90 million exit package on the way out. Once this series of events – the harassment complaint, the forced resignation, the lavish exit package – was publicly disclosed four years later (Wakabayashi & Benner, 2018), thousands of Google employees staged an orchestrated wave of walkouts from its worldwide offices one week later. Not coincidentally, one week after the walkouts, Google announced that it would be overhauling its sexual misconduct policy (Conger & Wakabayashi, 2018).

As another example, after complaints of sexual harassment by female employees against higher-level male executives at Nike, the athletic shoes and apparel seller, were being routinely ignored by human resources, a group of female employees took the matter into their own hands. They covertly surveyed other female Nike employees and discovered a litany of complaints. Somehow, a packet of the completed surveys landed on the Nike CEO's desk. Within weeks, at least six top male executives had either left Nike or announced that they would be leaving the company (Creswell et al., 2018). The group of departing executives included the head of diversity and inclusion, which makes me wonder exactly what he thought he was doing to make female employees feel more "included" at Nike. Also not coincidentally, one week after public reports of these events, the Nike CEO promised changes in how women would be treated in the company (Draper & Creswell, 2018).

These developments pose an issue of gender and leadership that demands our attention. They represent a gender issue because, although both men and women may engage in sexual harassment and be targets of it, most harassers are men and most targets are women (Fielden & Hunt, 2014; McDonald, 2012). They represent a leadership issue because they focus on a particularly problematic type of leader behavior; much of the sexual harassment that occurs is directed by leaders in positions of authority over lower-level employees (US Merit Systems Protection Board, 1995, 2018). However, sexual harassment by leaders of all genders directed toward people of all genders is problematic.

The purpose of this chapter is to examine sexual harassment by men in top management directed towards women. In it, I first consider legal and personal definitions of what constitutes sexual harassment. Next, I review theories and evidence for why some (but not all) men in top management sexually harass women. I then apply these theories to the saga of the man whose behavior and revelations about it set the stage for this chapter, Harvey Weinstein. Finally, I consider the implications of the Weinstein saga for dealing with sexual harassment by men in top management and for the long-term impact of the #MeToo movement.

LEGAL AND PERSONAL DEFINITIONS OF SEXUAL HARASSMENT

Definitions of sexual harassment have been incorporated into laws and guidelines worldwide (Clarke, 2007; McDonald, 2012). For example, in the United Kingdom, sexual harassment is defined as an illegal employment practice under the Equality Act 2010. According to Section 26 of the law (UK Government, 2010), sexual harassment occurs when a person (A) "engages in unwanted conduct of a sexual nature" towards another person (B), the conduct has the purpose or effect of "violating B's dignity or creating an intimidating, hostile, degrading, humiliating or offensive environment for B," and "because of B's rejection of or submission to the conduct, A treats B less favourably than A would treat B if B had not rejected or submitted to the conduct."

In the United States, sexual harassment is defined as an illegal employment practice under Title VII of the 1964 Civil Rights Act. According to guidelines issued by the US Equal Employment Opportunity Commission (2016), "Unwelcome sexual advances, requests for sexual favors, and other verbal or physical conduct of a sexual nature constitute sexual harassment when (1) submission to such conduct is made either explicitly or implicitly a term or condition of an individual's employment, (2) submission to or rejection of such conduct by an individual is used as the basis for employment decisions affecting such individual, or (3) such conduct has the purpose or effect of unreasonably interfering with an individual's work performance or creating an intimidating, hostile, or offensive working environment." An employer is held responsible for acts of sexual harassment when it knew or should have known of the conduct and failed to take corrective action.

The European Union (EU) established standards for what constitutes illegal sexual harassment within its member nations. According to its 2002 Equal Treatment Directive, sexual harassment is defined as "any form of unwanted verbal, nonverbal or physical conduct of a sexual nature with the purpose or effect of violating the dignity of a person, in particular when creating an intimidating, hostile, degrading, humiliating or offensive environment" (Zippel, 2009, p. 147). Although the directive allows latitude among EU members in deciding what specific behaviors constitute illegal sexual harassment, it has shaped the nature of members' legal approaches to sexual harassment (e.g., Saguy, 2018).

There is no universal legal definition of sexual harassment, and nation-specific definitions are subject to interpretation by the courts. Nonetheless, common themes that the behavior is unwanted and negatively impacts targets' work experiences and environments have emerged in legal definitions across nations (McDonald, 2012). Two types of sexual harassment have been generally recognized by courts as illegal, quid pro quo harassment and hostile environment harassment. In *quid pro quo sexual harassment*, the harasser asks the victim to participate in sexual activity in return for gaining a job, promotion, raise, or other reward. In *hostile environment sexual harassment*, the harasser directs unwanted sexually-oriented behavior toward the target and, in doing so, creates a hostile work environment (Cortina & Berdahl, 2008; O'Leary-Kelly et al., 2009).

Personal definitions as well as legal definitions of sexual harassment matter. Most people agree that some line needs to be drawn between acceptable and unacceptable sexually-oriented behavior in the workplace. However, it is impossible to draw a firm line that will be acceptable to all. For example, some types of sexually-oriented behavior at work (e.g., complimenting a coworker's appearance or attire) are welcomed by some people and considered sexual harassment by others, which presents courts with a challenge in enforcing sexual harassment laws when identical behavior may prompt such different reactions. Thus, from both a legal and an individual perspective, we need to consider which types of sexually oriented behavior people find most and least offensive, while recognizing that their judgments of exactly what behaviors constitute sexual harassment may vary (Berdahl & Aquino, 2009).

Sexually oriented behaviors that individuals may consider sexual harass-ment include verbal requests, verbal comments, and nonverbal displays. Spe-cific behaviors of each type are classified from more severe (presented first) to less severe. *Verbal requests* include sexual bribery (pressure for sexual favors with the threat or promise of reward), sexual advances (pressure for sexual favors with no threat or promise), relationship advances (repeated requests for an intimate relationship that is unwanted by the target), and more subtle advances (questions about one's sex life). *Verbal comments* include personally directed remarks (insulting jokes or comments made directly to the target), other-directed remarks (insulting jokes or comments about the target to oth-ers), and general sexual references. *Nonverbal displays* include sexual assault, sexual touching, sexual looks or gestures, and sexual materials (display of por-nography or other materials). Also, sexually oriented behavior is considered more severe when (1) the harasser is at a higher hierarchical level than the target, (2) the harasser has behaved similarly toward the target and others over time, and (3) there are job consequences for the target (Cortina & Berdahl, 2008; Fielden & Hunt, 2014; Gruber et al., 1996; McDonald, 2012).

Individuals' definitions of sexual harassment differ according to their per-sonal characteristics. The gender difference in definitions is strong. Men per-ceive a narrower range of behaviors as constituting sexual harassment and are more tolerant of sexual harassment than women (Rotundo et al., 2001). In addition, men are more likely than women to blame victims for their own har-assment (Jensen & Gutek, 1982). Further, individuals who rate higher on hos-tile sexism, which entails antagonism toward women as a group based on an ideology of male dominance and superiority (Fiske & Glick, 1995), are less likely to perceive sexual harassment (O'Connor et al., 2004).

Individuals' definitions of sexual harassment may also differ according to the characteristics of their organizational situations. For example, according to a survey of perceptions of sexual harassment across managerial levels (Col-lins & Blodgett, 1981), lower-level managers were more likely to see sexual harassment as a problem than middle-level managers. Further, top executives were the least likely to acknowledge the existence of sexual harassment and most likely to believe that the amount of sexual harassment at work is greatly exaggerated.

In summary, legal definitions of sexual harassment dictate legally acceptable standards of behavior in the workplace in various nations. However, individu-als' personal definitions of sexual harassment influence the kinds of sexually oriented behaviors they feel entitled to initiate and their responses to behaviors initiated by others. Individuals' definitions are in turn influenced by personal characteristics (e.g., gender, hostile sexism) and situational characteristics (e.g., managerial level). If men as a group and top executives as a group (who are overwhelmingly male) are least likely to "see" sexual harassment at work, we have an initial answer to the question posed in the chapter's title as to why some men in top management feel free to sexually harass women. They may not regard their behavior as sexual harassment even if others would disagree, but instead as reflecting normal work relations.

THEORIES OF SEXUAL HARASSMENT

In this section, I consider examples of person-centered, situation-centered, and social-system-centered theories, with confirming or disconfirming evidence when available, for why men in top management engage in sexual harassment directed towards women.

Person-centered theories

The *natural/biological model* of sexual harassment (Tangri et al., 1982), a person-centered theory, suggests that the phenomenon arises from individuals' basically sexual nature and represents a type of behavior to be accepted rather than a problem to be solved. People with strong sex drives are sexually aggressive toward others due to their natural and inevitable biological urges. Therefore, it is not surprising or of concern that some people exhibit sexual aggressiveness in work settings in the form of sexual harassment (Cortina & Berdahl, 2008).

Note that the natural/biological model is not necessarily limited to female–male work relations. According to Tangri et al.'s (1982, p. 35) original description of the model, an underlying assumption is "that men and women are naturally attracted to each other, that both sexes participate in sexually-oriented behavior in the workplace, and that they like it that way." In stating this assumption, they were treating gender as a binary variable and ignoring the possibility of same-gender attraction. If we assume instead that gender is a continuous variable as discussed in Chapter 1 (Hyde et al., 2019; Reilly, 2019) and acknowledge same-gender attraction, the natural/biological model suggests that people may act on both different-gender and same-gender attraction by exhibiting sexually aggressive behavior at work.

Survey evidence suggests that targets of sexual harassment at work are more likely than non-targets to be under the age of 35 and unmarried, which supports the natural/biological model if younger and unmarried employees are assumed to be the more sexually attractive and available (Tangri et al., 1982; US Merit Systems Protection Board, 1995). However, contrary to the natural/biological model's depiction of sexual harassment as not posing a problem to be solved, overwhelming research evidence suggests that the costs of sexual harassment are high. It has negative effects on employees' physical health (e.g., headaches, sleep disturbance, fatigue) and mental health (e.g., loss of self-esteem and self-confidence, anxiety, depression); even at low frequencies or low severity, sexual harassment exerts a significant negative impact on employees' job-related attitudes such as their sense of job satisfaction, organizational commitment, and feeling of involvement in their work (Bowling & Beehr, 2006; McDonald, 2012; McLaughlin et al., 2017; Willness et al., 2007). Further, it interferes with the functioning and performance of work teams and the organization as a whole (Raver & Gelfand, 2005). Thus, even if sexual harassment is regarded as natural and inevitable as the natural/biological model suggests, this does not mean that it represents harmless behavior.

Another person-centered theory, the *individual differences model* of sexual harassment, recognizes that some people engage in sexual harassment and others do not, even when they live and work under the same conditions (Pryor et al., 1995). Although most harassers are men, most men (and most women) are not harassers (O'Leary-Kelly et al., 2009). Individuals may vary widely in their likelihood to harass others. The individual differences model suggests personal factors that predict who is likely to engage in sexual harassment.

Individuals' tendencies to embrace hostile or benevolent sexism predict whether they will engage in sexual harassment. For example, male employees who are higher in hostile sexism (defined earlier) direct more severe types of sexual harassment toward female employees, thereby creating a hostile work environment for targets and their coworkers. However, male employees who are higher in benevolent sexism, which entails protectiveness toward women as a group as the "weaker gender," direct milder forms of sexual attention toward female employees in the belief that they are flattering the targets (Fiske & Glick, 1995).

Individuals' tendencies to view sexual harassment as unethical behavior (O'Leary-Kelly & Bowes-Sperry, 2001) may also predict whether they engage in it. When people view sexual harassment as involving more of an ethical or moral choice to be made, they would be expected to be less likely to engage in it. Several components of ethical issues have been identified (Jones, 1991) that seem relevant to individuals' decisions about whether to engage in sexual harassment. For example, if people expect that sexually-harassing behaviors would have minimal effects overall, would be unlikely to have negative effects, or would have few immediate effects, they may view sexual harassment as less of an ethical issue and be more likely to engage in it (O'Leary-Kelly & Bowes-Sperry, 2001).

Further, sexual harassment represents a type of aggressive behavior (O'Leary-Kelly et al., 2000), and individuals differ in their inclinations to be sexual aggressors. The confluence model of sexual aggression (Malamuth et al., 1995) proposes that sexually aggressive men are high on two dimensions, hostile masculinity (being insecure and defensive around women, gaining gratification from controlling or dominating them) and impersonal sex (having a noncommittal or game-playing orientation to sexual relations, which is different from having a strong sex drive). Men who are high on these two dimensions of sexual aggression would seem more likely to engage in sexual harassment than men who are low on one or both dimensions.

The individual differences model also suggests that some people are more likely to be targeted by sexual harassers than others. As noted earlier, most targets of sexual harassment are women (Fielden & Hunt, 2014; McDonald, 2012). However, there are individual differences among women in who are targeted by harassers.

For example, Berdahl (2007b) found that women who described themselves as high in masculinity on the Short Bem Sex-Role Inventory (Bem, 1981), regardless of their level of femininity, experienced more sexual harassment than those who described themselves as low in masculinity. She concluded that sexual harassment was being used as a way to punish "uppity" women who exhibited an abundance of masculine traits, thereby failing to conform to the female gender stereotype. These results were contrary to what the natural/biological model would predict, because sexual harassment was being directed towards women who were violating rather than meeting feminine ideals (Berdahl, 2007b).

Further, whether individuals are targeted by harassers is predicted by the intersection of their gender and race. A study of sexual harassment as well as ethnic harassment found that female employees experienced more sexual harassment than male employees, employees of color (i.e., who were members of racial and ethnic minority groups) experienced more ethnic discrimination than white employees, and women of color experienced more overall harassment than white men, white women, or men of color (Berdahl & Moore, 2006). These results support the "double whammy" perspective of the effects of the intersection of gender and race that was described in Chapter 4 (Bell et al., 1993; Nkomo, 1988), in this case pertaining to experiences of being targeted by harassers.

In summary, among the person-centered theories reviewed, the natural/biological model of sexual harassment has received minimal support. In contrast, the individual differences model of sexual harassment has received strong support, in that personal characteristics have been identified that predict who engages in sexual harassment and who is a target of sexual harassment. In particular, men in top management who are high in hostile and benevolent sexism, who are disinclined to view sexual harassment as an ethical issue, who are more sexually aggressive on the dimensions of hostile masculinity and impersonal sex, and who view women who do not meet feminine ideals as uppity may be the most likely to engage in sexual harassment.

Situation-centered theories

Organizations provide the situations, including structures and environments, in which most people work. Sexual harassment represents a significant problem in all types of organizations, including academic (Tenbrunsel et al., 2019), military (Fitzgerald et al., 1999), government (US Merit Systems Protection Board, 2018), and private-sector organizations (Ilies et al., 2003). However, according to the *organizational model* of sexual harassment (Tangri et al., 1982), certain organizational characteristics set the stage for its occurrence.

The hierarchical structure of most organizations sets the conditions under which employees gain access to and interact with each other. Organizational hierarchies grant higher-level employees position power over lower-level employees. With position power comes reward power, or the ability to offer favors to others who go along with one's wishes, and coercive power, or the ability to punish others who do not go along with one's wishes (Raven, 1993). Having reward and coercive power provides top-level managers the opportunity to engage in quid pro quo sexual harassment, because they may use the promise of rewards or the threat of punishments to obtain sexual gratification from others (Thacker & Ferris, 1991).

Power differentials may arise from other sources. For example, employees with critical expertise or information gain power over others independent of their position in the organizational hierarchy (Raven, 1993). Having expert and informational power also provides top-level managers the opportunity to engage in quid pro quo sexual harassment, because they may use the promise of sharing their valued expertise and information or the threat of withholding it to gain sexual gratification from others (Thacker & Ferris, 1991).

The organizational model suggests that sexual harassment is most prevalent in organizations with large power differentials. In support of this perspective, a meta-analysis of studies on sexual harassment in different types of organizations found that women in the military, a type of organization that emphasizes hierarchy-based power differentials, reported having experienced sexual harassment to a greater extent than women in universities, a type of organization that is characterized by smaller power differentials (Ilies et al., 2003).

Organizations differ in the extent to which their cultures tolerate sexual harassment (Hulin et al., 1996). They may (or may not) have policies and procedures in place that define sexual harassment and declare it as unacceptable behavior, policies may be strong (or weak) and enforced (or not), and managers at different levels may be intolerant (or tolerant) of sexual harassment; this set of actions or inactions collectively determines the organizational culture's tolerance for sexual harassment (Hulin et al., 1996). Hostile environment and quid pro quo sexual harassment are most likely to occur in organizational cultures that display a high tolerance for sexual harassment.

Organizations also differ in their ethical cultures (Shin, 2012). Strong ethical cultures promote adherence to ethical standards, whereas weak ethical cultures either tolerate or promote unethical behavior. In this vein, organizations with strong ethical cultures are likely to emphasize to employees that sexual harassment is unacceptable behavior and to deal with it when it occurs. In contrast, organizations with weak ethical cultures are likely to tolerate or ignore sexual harassment (Tenbrunsel et al., 2019). Top executives influence the ethical culture of their organizations through their own ethical (or lack of ethical) leadership (Shin, 2012).

Situations differ in the gender composition of the work environment at various levels, which may influence the occurrence of sexual harassment (Gutek, 1985). Women in male-dominated work environments, whether at the organizational or workgroup level, experience more sexual harassment than women in female-dominated environments (Berdahl, 2007b). In male-dominated environments, female victims of sexual harassment may be reluctant to come forward because they don't want to be labeled as troublemakers and put their careers at risk. Because the top management ranks are heavily skewed towards males, women stand out from the dominant gender and are treated differently (Kanter, 1977), which may include their being subjected to sexual harassment (Gutek, 1985).

Situations also differ in whether observers are present who would witness an incident of sexual harassment if it occurred but not be directly involved in it. According to what may be called the *observer-based model* of sexual harassment, quid pro quo sexual harassment is most likely to occur without observers present. However, in the case of hostile environment sexual harassment that directly affects the work environment, observers are more likely to be present (Bowes-Sperry & O'Leary-Kelly, 2005).

Observers of potential incidents of sexual harassment might prevent them from occurring by their very presence, on the assumption that most potential harassers would not like their behavior to be witnessed for fear of it coming back to haunt them. However, when sexual harassment occurs, observers are faced with a choice of whether to intervene to try to stop it or not (Bowes-Sperry & O'Leary-Kelly, 2005). Whether they actually intervene is likely to be influenced by the organizational culture's tolerance for sexual harassment, a situation-centered factor. It is also likely to be influenced by whether the observer perceives the behavior as representing an ethical issue (Bowes-Sperry & Powell, 1999; O'Leary-Kelly & Bowes-Sperry, 2001), a person-centered factor. Thus, the interaction between personal and situational factors may influence whether observers intervene in incidents of sexual harassment.

In summary, as a situation-centered theory, the organizational model of sexual harassment has received strong support. Several organizational charac-teristics, including the hierarchical structure and resulting power differentials, the culture regarding tolerance for sexual harassment and adherence to ethi-cal standards, and gender composition are likely to influence the occurrence of sexual harassment in their midst. In addition, the observer-based model of sexual harassment suggests that the presence of observers, and their actions if present, are likely to influence incidents of potential and actual sexual harassment.

Social-system-centered theories

The *sociocultural model* of sexual harassment (Tangri et al., 1982), a social-system-centered theory, depicts the phenomenon as a manifestation of patri-archal societies that expect men to be dominant and women to be compliant (Alvesson & Due Billing, 2009; Calás et al., 2014; Maier, 1999; Marshall, 1984). In such societies, sexual harassment may be regarded as a male prerogative with the purpose of preserving men's social status by keeping women economically dependent and subordinate (Berdahl, 2007a).

According to the sociocultural model, individuals with the least amount of power in society are the most likely to be harassed (Tangri et al., 1982). Power granted to men over women by societal processes is different from that granted by organizational hierarchies. Organizations vary in their emphasis on hierarchy and the magnitude of their power differentials. However, organizations operate within societal contexts, even multinational corporations with facilities located around the world, that are likely to influence their internal processes, including the level of sexual harassment exhibited within their boundaries.

Gender and sexuality represent intersecting social systems of power and dominance in the sociocultural model, with men using their sexual power to assert and sustain their dominance over women (Mackinnon, 1979; Uggen & Blackstone, 2004). In contrast, in the natural/biological model, gender and sexuality intersect in ways, including by fostering sexual harassment, that are natural and not necessarily problematic.

Further, due to the organizational construction of gender and sexuality, sexual harassment by heterosexual men "reinforces the power of men over women's bodies, paid jobs, reproductive labour and sexualities" (Hearn & Parkin, 1987, p. 132). Thus, sexual harassment represents an expression of power and dominance at the organizational level that is enabled by gendered and sexualized processes at the societal level. As a result, the three-way intersection between gender, sexuality, and organization may reflect societal cultures in ways that foster or tolerate sexual harassment (Burrell & Hearn, 1989; Hearn & Parkin, 1987).

According to what may be called the *national differences* model of sexual harassment, nations differ in values that influence the level of harassment within their boundaries. Luthar and Luthar (2002) proposed an influence of several dimensions of national culture identified by Hofstede (2001) on the occurrence and tolerance of sexual harassment.

For example, national cultures differ along Hofstede's (2001) individualism–collectivism dimension, which reflects the extent to which citizens value their self-interest versus the interests of their social group. People in individualist cultures are more inclined to question ethical standards set by their societies, whereas individuals in collectivist cultures are more likely to accept these standards (Luthar & Luthar, 2002). When sexual harassment is illegal behavior that violates societal norms, citizens are less likely to adhere to these norms in individualist than collectivist cultures. As a result, in individualist cultures, men's likelihood to sexually harass women and women's tolerance of unwanted sexually-oriented behaviors from men is likely to be greater than in collectivist cultures (Luthar & Luthar, 2002). Cross-cultural research with samples drawn from nations that differ along the individualism–collectivism dimension support this notion (Luthar & Luthar, 2007).

National cultures also differ along Hofstede's (2001) power distance dimension, which reflects the degree to which the culture tolerates social inequalities. Citizens feel freer to flaunt and take advantage of their power, whether societally granted or organizationally granted, in high power distance cultures than in low power distance cultures. As a result, in high power distance cultures, men's likelihood to sexually harass women and women's tolerance of unwanted sexually oriented behaviors from men is likely to be greater than in low power distance cultures (Luthar & Luthar, 2002). As above, cross-cultural research supports this notion (Luthar & Luthar, 2007).

Further, national cultures differ along Hostede's (2001) masculinity–femininity dimension, which refers to the extent of differences or inequalities in the roles assumed by women and men in a society, with a low masculinity (i.e., high femininity) culture promoting greater social equality between women and men. This dimension of national culture is similar to the GLOBE study's gender egalitarianism dimension (Emrich et al., 2004). A high-masculinity, low-gender egalitarianism culture is more likely to promote male aggressiveness towards and assertion of control over women, including by engaging in sexual harassment at work. In contrast, a low-femininity, high-gender egalitarianism culture is less likely to engage in gender discrimination (Emrich et al., 2004), with sexual harassment representing a distinct form of gender discrimination (MacKinnon, 1979). Accordingly, in high-masculinity, low-gender egalitarianism cultures, men's likelihood to sexually harass women and women's tolerance of unwanted sexually-oriented behaviors from men is likely to be greater than in low-masculinity, high-gender egalitarianism cultures (Luthar & Luthar, 2002).

In summary, among social-system-centered theories, the sociocultural model of sexual harassment incorporates the influence of patriarchal systems for which there is considerable supporting theory and evidence (Alvesson & Due Billing, 2009; Calás et al., 2014; Maier, 1999; Marshall, 1984). In addition, the national differences model of sexual harassment is supported by cross-cultural theory and evidence (Luthar & Luthar, 2002, 2007).

Thus, men in top management who display personal factors and behavioral tendencies associated with sexual harassment, work in organizational settings that tolerate or encourage such behaviors without the inconvenience of having potential witnesses present, and work in national cultures characterized by a high emphasis on power distance, individualism, and masculinity and a low emphasis on gender egalitarianism may be the most likely to engage in sexual harassment.

THE SAGA OF HARVEY WEINSTEIN

Next, I apply the definitions and theories of sexual harassment that have been reviewed to Harvey Weinstein, the man whose alleged behaviors were described at the beginning of the chapter. Weinstein may seem an outsize example of a man in top management who sexually harasses women. However, because so much has been revealed about his alleged behaviors and these revelations have had such widespread impact as seen in the overwhelming response to the #MeToo movement, talking about Weinstein seems a good place to start in considering why some men in top management feel free to sexually harass women. The analysis to follow is based on archival data and published reports (e.g., Kantor & Twohey, 2017, 2019; Ransom, 2020).

The behaviors

Consider the nature of the allegations against Weinstein in light of legal and personal definitions of sexual harassment. His alleged behaviors include quid pro quo and hostile environment sexual harassment, both of which are legally prohibited in many nations (Cortina & Berdahl, 2008; O'Leary-Kelly et al., 2009). They were at all levels of severity in personal definitions of sexual harassment, including verbal requests, verbal comments, and nonverbal displays of all types. Weinstein was at a higher hierarchical level than his targets, including lower-level employees and actresses hoping to be in his company's movies. He behaved in similar fashion toward more than 90 women over a period of decades (Ransom, 2020), and there were significant health and job consequences for the targets.

Thus, according to legal and personal definitions of sexual harassment, despite the fact that these definitions may differ between nations and between individuals, Weinstein's alleged behaviors represent those of a serial sexual harasser. However, I expect that Weinstein himself would disagree. Survey results reported earlier found that top executives were less likely to acknowledge the existence of sexual harassment than managers at lower levels (Collins & Blodgett, 1981). If Weinstein had completed the same survey, I expect that his view of sexual harassment would have been at the same level of denial or greater than other top executives.

The man

Person-centered theories of sexual harassment include the natural/biological model and the individual differences model. Weinstein was an older man who repeatedly directed unwanted sexually oriented behaviors towards younger women. If younger women are assumed to be more sexually attractive than older women, his behavior was consistent with the natural/biological model of sexual harassment (Tangri et al., 1982; US Merit Systems Protection Board, 1995).

Regarding the individual differences model, I am not going to speculate on whether Weinstein possessed any of the personal factors that have been identified as predictors of engaging in sexual harassment, including sexual aggressiveness (Malamuth et al., 1995) and hostile and benevolent sexism (Fiske & Glick, 1995). However, I do question his sense of ethics. It is unlikely that he regarded his sexually-oriented behaviors directed towards female targets as unethical (O'Leary-Kelly & Bowes-Sperry, 2001). Instead, these alleged behaviors reflect a striking sense of amorality regarding their likely negative consequences for his targets.

Thus, person-centered theories of sexual harassment provide a partial explanation for Weinstein's alleged behaviors.

The situation

As a situation-centered theory, the organizational model of sexual harassment suggests that organizational factors influence the extent to which sexual harassment occurs within an organization's boundaries. The situational context may also reflect the nature of the industry in which an organization does its business.

Consider the situation in which Weinstein's alleged behaviors occurred. His power and dominance over others was key. First, he was the co-founder of the company named after him, the Weinstein Company, which granted him power due to his pivotal role in its founding. Second, his being CEO of the company granted him the most position power of all employees. Third, his company was highly successful in the movie industry, gaining acclaim at film festivals and numerous awards for its movies and the actresses (and actors) in them. Fourth, he was highly visible in the industry – everyone knew who Harvey Weinstein was (Hall & Powell, 2017).

This situation created the context in which Weinstein's behavior was possible and he could get away with it. For a woman to cross Weinstein by rejecting his advances, especially if she was an aspiring actress, would be to risk her entire acting career. Not only could Weinstein punish her by keeping her out of his movies, he could also suggest to others in the industry that she is "difficult to work with" or otherwise slander her professional reputation, which could keep her career from ever getting started or taking off.

Thus, the organizational model of sexual harassment regarding the influence of power differentials provides an additional explanation for Weinstein's alleged behaviors. If he was not in such a strong power position that was reinforced by his company's hierarchy, his role as its co-founder and CEO, and his company's prominence in its industry, he might have engaged in the same types of behaviors but his female targets might not have felt as compelled to go along.

The social system

Social-system-centered theories of sexual harassment include the sociocultural model and the national differences model. According to the sociocultural model, sexual harassment is most likely to occur in patriarchal cultures (Alvesson & Due Billing, 2009; Calás et al., 2014; Maier, 1999; Marshall, 1984), including nations such as the US in which the Weinstein Company's headquarters were located; the alleged behaviors by Weinstein occurred either on company premises or on business trips such as to film festivals (Kantor & Twohey, 2019). Also, sexual harassment is most likely to be directed towards individuals with the least power in society (Tangri et al., 1982), such as the women targeted by Weinstein. The three-way intersection between gender, sexuality, and the Weinstein Company's organization reflected the societal culture in which his work was embedded so that he felt free to engage in sexual harassment of all types and levels of severity towards women (Burrell & Hearn, 1989; Hearn & Parkin, 1987).

According to the national differences model, dimensions of national culture influence the tolerance of sexual harassment. Among the dimensions of national culture proposed to have such an influence, the US was ranked first among all nations surveyed in individualism and below average in power distance (Hofstede, 2001). Further, the US was ranked above average in masculinity (Hofstede, 2001) and below average in gender egalitarianism (Emrich et al., 2004); low gender egalitarianism is roughly equivalent to high masculinity in national culture.

Thus, data from cross-cultural surveys most support the national differences model of sexual harassment with respect to the individualism–collectivism dimension of national culture. The US's being ranked first on Hofstede's (2001) individualism index suggests a high level and tolerance of sexual harassment in the nation in which the Weinstein Company was based. These data also offer moderate support for the influence of the masculinity–femininity and gender egalitarianism dimensions of national culture on the occurrence and tolerance of sexual harassment in the company's home nation. In contrast, little support is offered for the influence of the power distance dimension of national culture.

Overall, among social-system-centered theories of sexual harassment, the sociocultural model and the national differences model, especially regarding the individualism–collectivism dimension of national culture, provide a further explanation for Weinstein's alleged behaviors.

In summary, considering the saga of Harvey Weinstein, his alleged behaviors may be explained by person-centered, situation-centered, and social-system-centered theories of sexual harassment. I believe that situation-centered and social-system-centered theories based on power differentials in organizations and societies provide the strongest (i.e., most "powerful") explanations for how Weinstein was able to get away with what he did for so long.

CONCLUSIONS

In this section, I raise questions about the implications of the Weinstein saga and its aftermath and speculate about possible answers to these questions.

What would it take to suppress sexual harassment by men in top management?

Organizations are generally advised to take actions to discourage sexual harassment from occurring in their midst and to address it when it occurs; otherwise, they may be held in violation of the relevant laws in their nation. To do so, organizations need to adopt and enforce policies against sexual harassment and educate employees about the issue. Sexual harassment training programs need to discuss the reasons for the policies, the variety of forms of sexual harassment, and proper organizational responses to allegations of harassment, including formal investigatory procedures and actions to be taken depending on the severity of the alleged offense and the certainty that an offense was committed (Powell, 2019; Roehling & Huang, 2018).

That said, can you imagine a top-level executive who already engages in rampant sexual harassment (say Harvey Weinstein) going to a sexual harassment training program (say in the Weinstein Company) and being convinced by it to refrain from all future harassing behaviors? And can you imagine the same top-level executive's harassing behaviors, if a target of those behaviors filed a formal complaint, being thoroughly investigated and appropriately penalized by the human resources department whose manager is likely to report directly or indirectly to the harasser? No, neither can I. In major corporations, virtually all men at lower levels have learned that even if they are inclined to harass women, they risk their employment and livelihood if caught. Men at the top, if they are so inclined, play by different rules (Hall & Powell, 2017), and sexual harassment policies and training programs are unlikely to curb their behavior.

However, corporate CEOs answer to boards of directors, which have the power to fire them at will. In the case of Harvey Weinstein, although some board members were aware of the allegations against him in advance, the all-male board took no action until after the allegations became public knowledge (Kantor & Twohey, 2017, 2019).

Would the Weinstein Company's board of directors have acted differently if it had had at least one female member and she (or they) had learned about the allegations prior to their being publicly revealed? A research study conducted in Norway, a nation with an expansive gender quota mandate for boards of directors (Hughes et al., 2017), suggests a possible answer to this question.

Wang & Kelan (2013) found that the percentage of female members on a board of directors, as well as the board having a "critical mass" (at least three) of female directors, were positively related to the board having a female chair; further, all of these factors were positively related to the company having a female CEO. Overall, these results suggest that having more women on a board of directors, particularly in the board chair role, increases the likelihood of it having a female CEO (Wang & Kelan, 2013).

These results raise the question of what difference it would have made if the co-founder and CEO of the Weinstein Company had been Hannah Weinstein instead of Harvey Weinstein. I can imagine two possible outcomes. First, the likelihood of the CEO engaging in sexual harassment would have been affected. Considering the implications of the person-centered, situation-centered, and social-system-centered theories reviewed as a whole, I believe that Hannah would have been less likely than Harvey to engage in rampant sexual harassment.

Second, the likelihood of the CEO promoting an organizational culture that tolerated sexual harassment would have been affected. Considering gender differences in personal definitions (Rotundo et al., 2001) and experiences (O'Leary-Kelly et al., 2009) of sexual harassment as well as the numbers of powerful men versus powerful women who have been brought down by the #MeToo movement (Carlsen et al., 2018), I believe that Hannah would have been more inclined than Harvey to promote an organizational culture that showed zero tolerance for sexual harassment and dealt with it promptly when it occurred.

What will be the long-term impact of the #MeToo movement?

The #MeToo movement may have both positive and negative effects in the long run. On the one hand, its long-term effects will be positive if men in power inclined to engage in sexual harassment become less likely to do so because of fear of having their behavior receive public attention and damage their careers (Johnson et al., 2019). Such fear would be legitimate. In the year after the Weinstein allegations, more than 200 powerful men lost their jobs after public allegations of sexual harassment (and nearly half of their replacements were women). In contrast, in the year before the allegations, less than 30 powerful men were reported to have resigned or been fired after public allegations of sexual harassment (Carlsen et al., 2018). Also, despite having to process difficult emotions, the support women receive after tweeting about their experiences of sexual harassment may be beneficial as a demonstration of solidarity (Mendes et al., 2018); it may also help to increase their feelings of self-esteem and decrease their feelings of self-doubt (Johnson et al., 2019).

On the other hand, the movement's long-term effects will be negative if well-meaning men in power become reluctant to mentor lower-level women, which would help the women to advance in their careers, because of fear that their good intentions may be misinterpreted (Bennhold, 2019). One male executive said when interviewed at a conference, "I now think twice about spending one-on-one time with a young female colleague." He spoke only under the condition of anonymity because he regarded the topic as "just too sensitive." An anonymous male colleague said in response, somewhat ironi- cally, "Me, too" (Bennhold, 2019). Men may also be more reluctant to hire attractive women, especially for jobs that require close interpersonal interac- tions with men (Atwater et al., 2019).

Further, just as the intersection of gender and race influences whether individuals are targeted by sexual harassers (Berdahl & Moore, 2006), it may also influence who feels included in the #MeToo movement (Onwuachi-Willig, 2018). The movement was launched by a black woman, Tarana Burke, before hashtags existed. However, the hashtag movement of the same name that was launched by a white actress, Alyssa Milano, has received far greater attention. One criticism of the #MeToo movement is that it represents another example of the "whitewashing" of a feminist movement when brought into mainstream conversation. Onwuachi-Willig (2018, p. 105) raised a question that women of color may ask, "What about #UsToo?" All women's experiences of sexual harassment by powerful men deserve attention, not only the experiences of women of a particular race.

In conclusion, sexual harassment by some, but not all, men in top man- agement directed toward less powerful women represents an important and disturbing linkage between gender and leadership. It focuses on a particularly troubling type of leader behavior that, when it occurs, causes considerable harm for its victims.

What would it take to reduce the phenomenon of sexual harassment in the executive suite? As the chapter suggests, public exposure of further wrong-doing of this type by people in power would help. Prompt and decisive actions by corporate boards of directors would help. Continuation of the #MeToo movement in a manner in which all victims of sexual harassment feel included would help. Finally, based on the discussion of what Hannah Weinstein would have done differently from Harvey Weinstein, I believe that having more female CEOs, the numbers of whom are very small (see Chapter 3), would help.

6

WHAT ACTIONS WOULD WORK TOWARD UNDOING THE LINKAGE BETWEEN GENDER AND LEADERSHIP?

In Chapter 1, I laid out a positive scenario for the roles that women vis-à-vis men will play in the workplace of the future, one in which they are treated according to the human capital they bring to the job – knowledge, skills, abilities, education, relevant work experience, past performance, and so on (Stumpf & London, 1981) – and given the chance to reach their leadership potential regardless of their gender. I first articulated a version of such a scenario in the first edition of *Women and Men in Management* (Powell, 1988). More than three decades later, I still believe that achieving such a scenario represents an appropriate goal. In this chapter, I consider steps that can be taken toward achieving this goal.

Many of the theories that have been presented in this book focus on what keeps us from achieving this goal. For example, social-system-centered theories primarily focus on how social systems become "gendered" or "do gender" (Acker, 1990; Calás & Smircich, 1996; Ridgeway, 1991; Risman, 2004; West & Zimmerman, 1987) so that gender is established and maintained as a central organizing principle in social relations. In comparison, relatively little attention has been given to how social systems may become "ungendered" or "undo gender" (Deutsch, 2007; Kelan, 2018; Risman, 2009). Deutsch (2007, p. 108) observed that West & Zimmerman's (1987) approach to doing gender implied that "if gender is constructed, then it can be deconstructed." However, the notion of doing gender has been mostly used as a theory of gender conformity or maintenance, with resistance to the gendering of social systems often dismissed as futile (Deutsch, 1987). For example, Kelan's (2018, p. 550) review of the literature on how men do or undo gender in organizations identified 35 practices by which men do gender and only nine practices by which they undo gender. This reported imbalance may be because men are more engaged in doing than undoing gender as theories and research on patriarchal systems suggest (Alvesson & Due Billing, 2009; Calás et al., 2014; Maier, 1999; Marshall, 1984). However, as Kelan (2018) suggested, it may also be because how men undo gender at work is under-examined compared with how they do gender.

Doing gender has been conceptualized as creating gender differences, whereas undoing gender has been conceptualized as reducing gender differences (Deutsch, 2007; Kelan, 2018). Adapting these conceptualizations to the linkage between gender and leadership and consistent with the goal of working towards achieving the positive scenario stated above, I define "undoing the linkage between gender and leadership" as increasing the treatment of women and men with respect to leader roles according to their human capital and decreasing such treatment according to their gender. In contrast, I define "doing the linkage between gender and leadership" as increasing or reinforcing the treatment of women and men with respect to leader roles according to their gender and decreasing or minimizing such treatment according to their human capital. Conceptualized in these terms, I believe that the appropriate goal is to work toward undoing the linkage between gender and leadership.

This is not to say that the linkage between gender and leadership can be completely undone. Theories of why gender differences occur in the first place have invoked the influence of both "nature" (e.g., biological forces that are less amenable to change) and "nurture" (e.g., environmental forces that may be resistant to but are more amenable to change; Eagly & Wood, 2013). Theories of gender differences based on the influence of nature (Archer & Lloyd, 2002; Eagly & Wood, 2013; Lippa, 2005) are generally compatible with person-centered theories of the linkage between gender and leadership, in that personal factors influence the human capital that people bring to leader roles. In contrast, theories of gender differences based on the influence of nurture (Eagly & Wood, 2013; Lippa, 2005; Martin & Ruble, 2009) are generally compatible with situation-centered and social-system-centered theories of the linkage between gender and leadership, in that both situational and social system factors influence the nature of the work environments within which leadership occurs. Although scholars have debated whether nature or nurture is more important in shaping social behavior, the debate seems misguided. Indeed, nature and nurture are likely to intersect to influence the linkage between gender and leadership (Eagly & Wood, 2013).

To wrap up the book, I offer several examples of actions that would seem likely to work toward undoing the linkage between gender and leadership that has been documented in earlier chapters. Chapter 1 served as an introduction, and Chapters 2 through 5 primarily focused on theories and research regarding major questions about the linkage between gender and leadership. The focus of this chapter is on personal, situational, and social system factors that may be amenable to change that would move us closer to achieving the desired goal.

DEBIASING

Individuals' cognitive processes, whether they are making decisions about who attains leader roles, reacting to leaders of their own, using their power as leaders, or overseeing the actions of other leaders, represent personal factors that underlie some of the explanations offered for the linkage between gender and leadership in Chapters 2 through 5.

For example, Chapter 2 describes stereotyping, or the classification of people into groups and the attribution of different personal characteristics to different groups (Fiske, 1998; Hilton & Von Hippel, 1996), as a basic cognitive activity. The chapter proceeds to examine the linkage between widely-held gender stereotypes (Ellemers, 2018; Kite et al., 2008) and leader stereotypes (Powell & Butterfield, 1979, 1989; Powell et al., 2002). However, people may differ in the extent to which they personally endorse gender and leader stereotypes.

Chapter 2 also considers change that may occur in individuals' gender and leader stereotypes in the presence of disconfirming information (Hilton & Von Hippel, 1996; Rothbart, 1981). However, individuals' cognitive processes are subject to biases that influence whether they recognize that new information contradicts their previously formed stereotypes. People may display inattentional bias, or the tendency to not see what they are not looking for (Bazerman & Moore, 2013; Mack, 2003). They may also display change blindness, or the inability to detect changes in their environment, especially if these changes are gradual rather than abrupt (Bazerman & Moore, 2013; Rothbart, 1981; Simons & Rensink, 2005). Both types of bias reinforce the durability of gender and leader stereotypes over time.

Chapter 3 considers decision-makers' cognitive processes that affect their promotions to top management; such decisions are most prone to biases because they rely the least on objective credentials (Antal & Krebsbach-Gnath, 1988). Decision-makers' personal endorsement of gender and leader stereotypes is likely to influence their promotion decisions for top management positions. Gender-based jobholder schemas, or mental models of the ideal jobholder, may also influence their promotion decisions (Perry et al., 1994). Although Chapter 3 focuses on promotions to top management, similar cognitive processes may influence decisions about who is selected for or promoted to managerial positions at all levels.

Chapter 4 considers individuals' cognitive processes when they establish a preference for reporting to a female or male boss; such preferences reflect a form of bias. However, having had a female boss, a situational factor, may dispel subordinates' biases against women as bosses in general, a personal factor (Bhatnagar & Swamy, 1995; Ezell et al., 1981). Individuals may also display an overconfidence bias by believing too strongly in the accuracy of their own beliefs (Bazerman & Moore, 2013), which men have been found to possess in their beliefs about their own leadership abilities (Paustian-Underdahl et al., 2014; Reuben et al., 2012).

Chapter 5 considers individuals' cognitive processes as they establish their own definitions of sexual harassment, which are associated with personal factors such as gender (Rotundo et al., 2001) and hostile sexism (O'Connor et al., 2004). The cognitive processes of members of corporate boards of directors may influence whether they tolerate sexual harassment by top executives or take decisive action against it (Kantor & Twohey, 2019). Further, board members' cognitive processes may influence whether they favor the appointment of female CEOs (Wang & Kelan, 2013), who would seem less likely than male CEOs to engage in or tolerate sexual harassment in the first place.

Thus, individuals' cognitive processes, whether they occupy a managerial, subordinate, or board director role, have a considerable influence on the linkage between gender and leadership. These processes may be subject to biases that lead to distorted judgments about others. The challenge that people face is "to avoid the biases that arise from being a prisoner of one's present perspective" (Fischhoff, 1982, p. 319). Individuals will always engage in some form of cognitive processes in relation to leader roles, but we have reason to be concerned when these processes are biased in any way.

What can be done about biased cognitive processes? Debiasing, or the reduction or elimination of biases from the cognitive strategies of decision-makers, would help (Bazerman & Moore, 2013; Fischhoff, 1982; Larrick, 2004). Training in decision-making that warns about the possibility of biased judgements, describes the nature of potential biases, provides specific feedback, and is supplemented by personal coaching contributes to debiasing (Fischhoff, 1982). Human resources directors may promote the implementation of such training for key decision-makers in their organizations, with the training representing a situational factor. Also, decision-makers may seek out such training themselves, with their debiasing strategies representing personal factors to improve their own cognitive processes. Further, debiasing training may be offered to all employees to reduce biases that affect social relations at work, including relations between leaders and subordinates.

Whether initiated by individuals or organizations, the adoption of debiasing strategies works toward undoing the linkage between gender and leadership. Effective debiasing decreases reliance on personal biases in all leadership-related phenomena on the basis of gender as well as other personal character-istics such as race, ethnicity, sexual orientation, national origin, socioeconomic class, and so on.

LEADERSHIP TRAINING

Chapter 4 reports meta-analytic results suggesting that female leaders are higher in behaviors that contribute to leader effectiveness (e.g., all dimensions of transformational leadership, contingent reward dimension of transactional leadership) and lower in behaviors that detract from leader effectiveness (e.g., passive management by exception dimension of transactional leadership, laissez-faire leadership) than male leaders (Eagly et al., 2003; Judge & Piccolo, 2004; Lowe et al., 1996; Wang et al., 2011). These gender differences in leadership style may be influenced by personal factors that in turn are the result of nature, nurture, or the intersection of nature and nurture (Eagly & Wood, 2013). They may also be influenced by situational factors such as the gender composition of the organizational setting and the nature of the leader role (Eagly et al., 1995).

Further, gender differences in leadership style may be influenced by social system factors. Due to gendered social-system-centered processes, female leaders may feel pressured to conform to the feminine gender stereotype, with which transformational leadership is most congruent, whereas male leaders feel pressured to conform to the masculine gender stereotype, with which transformational leadership is less congruent (Bass et al., 1996; Kark, 2004).

Leadership training, a situational factor, may work toward undoing this linkage between gender and leadership. Training programs have been found to promote *all* leaders displaying leadership styles such as transformational leadership that are regarded to be effective (Parry & Sinha, 2005). If the training is effective in itself, it may achieve the desirable result of increasing overall leader effectiveness.

PROCEDURES FOR FILLING MANAGERIAL POSITIONS

Chapter 3 describes the work setting in which Tony Butterfield and I (1994) conducted research on the glass ceiling phenomenon, the US government. In making decisions about which applicants are promoted to nonpolitical top management positions, this organization uses procedures that emphasize procedural fairness (Greenberg, 1990) in several ways. First, open top management positions are publicly announced. Second, all decisions are made using the exact same procedure. Third, detailed records are kept at all stages of the decision-making process, including ratings of applicants' credentials and decisions about whether to advance the application of each applicant to the next stage, and retained for at least two years. Thus, the procedure by which promotion decisions for top management are made in this organization is structured, standardized, and available for review (Powell & Butterfield, 1994, 2015b).

The collection and retention of promotion records makes it possible for government officials to identify decisions that do not appear to have been properly made, e.g., when ratings of applicants' credentials are not aligned with decisions about whether they advance to the next stage of the decision-making process or ultimately get the job. Although such procedures cannot prevent biases from entering into decision-makers' ratings and decisions, they provide incentives for decision-makers not to make their biases known in ways that could be identified by review of promotion records. In this way, decision-makers may be held accountable for their decisions (Powell & Butterfield, 1994, 2015b).

Such procedures represent situational factors that work toward undoing the linkage between gender and leadership by focusing decision-makers' attention on applicants' human capital rather than their gender. Work organizations could learn from the US government by adapting such procedures to meet their own needs for filling managerial positions rather than shrouding their procedures in secrecy, the more common practice. Further, although Tony and I focused on the outcomes of promotion procedures for top management positions in our research (Powell & Butterfield, 1994), similar procedures could be used to fill managerial positions at all organizational levels.

ORGANIZATIONAL CULTURE REGARDING WORK HOURS AND AVAILABILITY

Chapter 3 describes an organizational culture that requires long work hours and 24/7 availability for managers (Ferguson et al., 2016; Milliken & Dunn-Jensen, 2005) as an alternative explanation for the "opt-out revolution" (Belkin, 2003; Kuperberg & Stone, 2008) that was attributed to women's lack of aspirations to top management. I regard an organizational culture that expects managers to work unrelentingly long hours and put their family life on hold whenever a work need arises as abusive (Powell, 1998). Such an organizational culture operates with callous disregard for its managers, not even displaying what might be considered a minimum amount of concern for their human needs.

An abusive organizational culture regarding work hours and availability may offer a manager ways to mitigate work demands such as flexible work arrangements and other family-supportive programs (Greenhaus & Powell, 2017). However, taking advantage of flexible work arrangements often invokes a flexibility stigma (Williams et al., 2013), such that managers who request flexibility are seen as less committed to the job and organization than managers who do not request it. Such arrangements are generally regarded as more for women than men in an organizational culture that largely reflects the beliefs of men, and requesting to use them is (mistakenly) seen as a lack of commitment to the job and organization, thereby maintaining gender differences in career advancement (Ely & Padavic, 2020; Padavic et al., 2020). If an organization has an abusive culture regarding work hours and availability, it can offer all the family-supportive programs it wants and brag about how family-supportive it is, but the reality is something different (Powell, 1998, 2019).

Thus, an abusive organizational culture represents a situational factor that contributes to doing the linkage between gender and leadership. In contrast, a family-supportive organizational culture works towards undoing the linkage between gender and leadership. It does not expect that managers will constantly prioritize work over family through working long hours and being available 24/7, and it does not impose career penalties on managers who choose not to do so (Greenhaus & Powell, 2017). Managers in family-supportive cultures are more likely to take advantage of family-supportive programs that help them to meet their full range of human needs without fear of reprisal (Greenhaus & Powell, 2017). Being family-supportive is only one way in which an organization's culture may influence the nature of the linkage between gender and leadership within its boundaries.

ORGANIZATIONAL CULTURE REGARDING EQUAL EMPLOYMENT OPPORTUNITY

Chapter 4 considers the potential and actual impact of equal employment opportunity (EEO) laws that have been enacted in many nations (Archibong & Sharps, 2013; Crosby et al., 2006; Davies & Robison, 2016; Konrad & Linnehan, 1999). Although EEO laws vary across nations, they share the general objective of banning employment discrimination on the basis of gender as well as other selected personal characteristics.

However, EEO laws may achieve this objective only if organizations adhere to them, either voluntarily or due to enforcement. As Chapter 4 noted, organizations may vary widely in their EEO culture, a situational factor. Some organizations would embrace the notion of equal employment opportunity as a smart business practice even if there were no EEO laws. Other organizations minimally comply with EEO laws for the purpose of avoiding costly lawsuits or damage to their reputations rather than believing in the spirit of the laws. Still other organizations blatantly ignore EEO laws in the belief that the laws are misguided and will or should not be enforced (Pati, 1977; Powell, 2019).

Thus, the passage and enforcement of EEO laws, social system factors, create the potential for working toward undoing of the linkage between gender and leadership. However, organizational EEO cultures, a situational factor, determine the extent to which the laws actually contribute to the undoing of this linkage.

ORGANIZATIONAL CULTURE REGARDING SEXUAL HARASSMENT

Chapter 5 considers how organizational cultures regarding sexual harassment, a situational factor, may vary. A strong culture is intolerant of sexual harassment, has policies against it that are strictly enforced, and regularly reminds employees that it represents unacceptable behavior. In contrast, a weak culture ignores or dismisses sexual harassment as unworthy of attention and thereby allows it to flourish; if employees are inclined to harass others in a weak culture regarding sexual harassment, they may do so without fear of reprisal (Hulin et al., 1996). An organization's culture is in turn influenced by its ethical culture, with weak ethical cultures more likely to tolerate or ignore sexual harassment than strong ethical cultures (Tenbrunsel et al., 2019).

Thus, organizational cultures regarding sexual harassment, a situational factor, may contribute to doing or undoing the linkage between gender and leadership. Organizational cultures in general are subject to influence by top executives (Shin, 2012). For example, if an organization's CEO engages in sexual harassment or tolerates it by others, the organizational culture is likely to follow. In contrast, if its CEO refrains from sexual harassment and ensures that strong policies are in place against it, the organizational culture is also likely to follow. CEOs and other members of top management teams do not fully determine organizational cultures regarding sexual harassment, managerial work hours and availability, equal employment opportunity, or other aspects of work. However, they may have a strong influence on their organization's culture through their actions or inactions.

PROACTIVE BOARDS OF DIRECTORS

Chapter 5, in discussing the saga of Harvey Weinstein, noted that the all-male board of directors of the Weinstein Company failed to take any action against him until allegations of his rampant sexual harassment became public knowledge, even though many of the board members had learned of these allegations beforehand (Kantor & Twohey, 2019). In the wake of the #MeToo movement, boards of directors of many publicly traded firms have learned that sexual harassment scandals may cause trouble for them too (Morrissey, 2018).

Among the responsibilities of boards of directors include control and service roles (Johnson et al., 1996). The board's control role consists of monitoring top managers' behaviors, including hiring and firing the CEO and other top managers, and otherwise overseeing their behavior to ensure that stockholders' interests are being met. Its service role consists of advising the CEO and top managers and actively encouraging corporate strategies on managerial issues that will benefit stockholders' interests (Johnson et al., 1996). When stockholders perceive that the board is not adequately representing their interests, they may express their displeasure in ways that go beyond simply selling their shares or protesting at annual stockholders' meetings.

For example, stockholders may sue the board for breaching its fiduciary duties by failing to avoid or address sexual harassment scandals (Morrissey, 2018). This was the case for 21st Century Fox, the parent company of Fox News, which settled such a lawsuit (Stempel, 2017) after multiple allegations of sexual harassment against Fox News' CEO Roger Ailes (Carlson, 2016; Redden, 2016) were followed by multiple allegations against television host Bill O'Reilly (Steel & Schmidt, 2017), both of whom received large severance packages upon their departure. Although Ailes resigned under pressure and O'Reilly was fired by Ailes's successor as CEO, the board was sued for not making itself aware of or properly addressing Fox News' highly sexualized environment that fostered rampant sexual harassment until it was publicly exposed.

In the wake of sexual harassment allegations or scandals, corporate boards of directors may work towards undoing the linkage between gender and leadership through their actions, or maintaining this linkage through their inaction. I believe that board concerns should go beyond avoiding lawsuits by targets of sexual harassers or stockholders. Boards of directors may act proactively in their control role by addressing sexual harassment by the CEO and top managers promptly and decisively if it occurs, and they may act proactively in their service role by encouraging strong organizational cultures that show zero tolerance for such behavior (Morrissey, 2018); both types of actions will benefit employees as well as stockholders. Further, as Chapter 5 suggests, boards may be able to avoid such allegations and scandals by hiring female CEOs, who would seem less likely to tolerate sexual harassment or engage in it.

CONCLUSIONS

The linkage between gender and leadership is complex and multifaceted. It varies according to personal, situational, and social system factors. It is subject to change, and has changed in some ways, over time as the players themselves change and as the situational and societal contexts in which it is enacted evolve.

Looking forward, I expect to see both stability and change in various aspects of the linkage between gender and leadership. To make sense of the stability and change that occurs, I recommend further theory and research on, but not limited to, the questions about this linkage addressed in Chapters 2 through 5. I also recommend further theory and research on the effects of various actions by different parties on undoing the relationship between gender and leadership, including but not limited to the examples of actions described in this chapter. Overall, future scholarly attention to the ways in which people, organizations, and societies both do and undo gender in relation to leadership is needed.

With such scholarly attention, and such actions, hopefully progress will be made toward undoing the linkage between gender and leadership, so that all individuals are treated according to the human capital they bring to the workplace and given full opportunity to reach their leadership potential regardless of their gender. Speaking optimistically, I very much look forward to seeing such progress.

REFERENCES

Acker, J. (1990). Hierarchies, jobs, bodies: A theory of gendered organizations. *Gender & Society, 4*, 139–158.

Acker, J. (1998). The future of "gender and organizations": Connections and boundaries. *Gender, Work and Organization, 5*, 195–206.

Acker, J. (2006). Inequality regimes: Gender, class, and race in organizations. *Gender & Society, 20*, 441–464.

Adamson, M., & Kelan, E. K. (2019). "Female heroes": Celebrity executives as postfemininst role models. *British Journal of Management, 30*, 981–996.

Ahl, H. (2006). Why research on women entrepreneurs needs new directions. *Entrepreneurship Theory & Practice, 30*, 595–621.

Alimo-Metcalfe, B. (2010). Developments in gender and leadership: Introducing a new "inclusive" model. *Gender in Management: An International Journal, 25*, 630–639.

Alvesson, M., & Due Billing, Y. (2009). *Understanding Gender and Organizations*, 2nd ed. London: Sage.

American Psychological Association. (2018). *APA Guidelines for the Psychological Practice with Boys and Men*. Washington, DC: American Psychological Association.

Antal, A. B., & Krebsbach-Gnath, C. (1988). Women in management: Unused resources in the Federal Republic of Germany. In N. J. Adler & D. N. Izraeli (eds.), *Women in Management Worldwide* (pp. 141–156). Armonk, NY: Sharpe.

Archer, J., & Lloyd, B. (2002). *Sex and Gender*, 2nd ed. Cambridge: Cambridge University Press.

Archibong, U., & Sharps, P. W. (2013). A comparative analysis of affirmative action in the United Kingdom and United States. *Journal of Psychological Issues in Organizational Culture, 3* (S1), 28–49.

Arifeen, S. R., & Gatrell, G. (2020). Those glass chains that bind you: How British Muslim women professionals experience career, faith and family. *British Journal of Management, 31*, 221–236.

Atwater, L. A., Tringale, A. M., Sturm, R. E., Taylor, S. N., & Braddy, P. W. (2019). Looking ahead: How what we know about sexual harassment now informs us of the future. *Organizational Dynamics, 48* (4), 1–9.

Ball, F. (2019, August 22). More Steves than women are FTSE 100 CEOs. *Economia*. Retrieved September 17, 2019, from https://economia.icaew.com.

Baron, J. N., Davis-Blake, A., & Bielby, W. T. (1986). The structure of opportunity: How promotion ladders vary within and among organizations. *Administrative Science Quarterly*, *31*, 248–273.

Bartol, K. M. (1978). The sex structuring of organizations: A search for possible causes. *Academy of Management Review*, *3*, 805–815.

Bartol, K. M., & Butterfield, D. A. (1976). Sex effects in evaluating leaders. *Journal of Applied Psychology*, *61*, 446–454.

Bass, B. M. (1985). *Leadership and Performance beyond Expectations*. New York: Free Press.

Bass, B. M. (1998). *Transformational Leadership: Industry, Military, and Educational Impact*. Mahwah, NJ: Erlbaum.

Bass, B. M., Avolio, B. J., & Atwater, L. (1996). The transformational and transactional leadership of men and women. *Applied Psychology: An International Review*, *45* (1), 5–34.

Bazerman, M. H., & Moore, D. (2013). *Judgment in Managerial Decision Making*, 8th ed. Hoboken, NJ: Wiley.

Becker, G. S. (1971). *The Economics of Discrimination*, 2nd ed. Chicago: University of Chicago Press.

Belkin, L. (2003, October 26). The opt-out revolution. *New York Times*. Retrieved September 9, 2010, from www.nytimes.com.

Bell, E. L., Denton, T. C., & Nkomo, S. (1993). Women of color in management: Toward an inclusive analysis. In E. A. Fagenson (ed.), *Women in Management: Trends, Issues, and Challenges in Managerial Diversity* (pp. 105–130). Newbury Park, CA: Sage.

Bem, S. L. (1974). The measurement of psychological androgyny. *Journal of Consulting and Clinical Psychology*, *42*, 155–162.

Bem, S. L. (1981). *Bem Sex-Role Inventory: Professional Manual*. Palo Alto, CA: Consulting Psychologists Press.

Bem, S. L. (1993). *The Lenses of Gender: Transforming the Debate on Sexual Inequality*. New Haven, CT: Yale University Press.

Bennhold, K. (2019, January 27). Another side of #MeToo: Male managers fearful of mentoring women. *New York Times*. Retrieved January 28, 2019, from www.nytimes.com.

Berdahl, J. L. (2007a). Harassment based on sex: Protecting social status in the context of gender hierarchy. *Academy of Management Review*, *32*, 641–658.

Berdahl, J. L. (2007b). The sexual harassment of uppity women. *Journal of Applied Psychology*, *92*, 425–437.

Berdahl, J. L., & Aquino, K. (2009). Sexual behavior at work: Fun or folly? *Journal of Applied Psychology*, *94*, 34–47.

Berdahl, J. L., & Moore, C. (2006). Workplace harassment: Double jeopardy for minority women. *Journal of Applied Psychology*, *91*, 426–436.

Bhatnagar, D., & Swamy, R. (1995). Attitudes toward women as managers: Does interaction make a difference? *Human Relations*, *48*, 1285–1307.

Binard, F. (2017). The British Women's Liberation Movement in the 1970s: Redefining the personal and political. *Revue Française de Civilisation Brittanique, XXII-Hors série*, 1–17 (aka *French Journal of British Studies*).

Bowes-Sperry, L., & O'Leary-Kelly, A. M. (2005). To act or not to act: The dilemma faced by observers of sexual harassment. *Academy of Management Review, 30*, 288–306.

Bowes-Sperry, L., & Powell, G. N. (1999). Observers' reactions to social-sexual behavior at work: An ethical decision making perspective. *Journal of Management, 25*, 779–802.

Bowleg, L. (2008). When Black + lesbian + woman ≠ Black lesbian woman: The methodological challenges of qualitative and quantitative intersectionality research. *Sex Roles, 59*, 312–325.

Bowling, N. A., & Beehr, T. A. (2006). Workplace harassment from the victim's perspective: A theoretical model and meta-analysis. *Journal of Applied Psychology, 91*, 998–1012.

Boyce, L. A., & Herd, A. M. (2003). The relationship between gender role stereotypes and requisite military leadership characteristics. *Sex Roles, 49*, 365–378.

Brady, K. (2012). *Strong Woman: Ambition, Grit, and a Great Pair of Heels*. London: Harper Collins.

Breen, R., & Cooke, L. P. (2005). The persistence of the gendered division of domestic labour. *European Sociological Review, 21*, 43–57.

Brenan, M. (2017, November 16). Americans no longer prefer male boss to female boss. *Gallup News Service*. Retrieved November 20, 2017, from www.news.gallup.com.

Broadbridge, A., & Hearn, J. (2008). Gender and management: New directions in research and continuing patterns in practice. *British Journal of Management, 19*, S38–S49.

Broadbridge, A., & Simpson, R. (2011). 25 years on: Reflecting on the past and looking to the future in gender and management research. *British Journal of Management, 22*, 470–483.

Brooke-Marciniak, B., & Schreiber, U. (2015, March 3). The real story: There are not enough women CEOs. *Forbes*. Retrieved September 18, 2019, from www.forbes.com

Broverman, I. K., Vogel, S. R., Broverman, D. M., Clarkson, F. E., & Rosenkrantz, P. S. (1972). Sex role stereotypes: A current appraisal. *Journal of Social Issues, 28* (2), 59–78.

Bryant, A. (2009, July 26). No doubt: Women are better managers. *New York Times*. Retrieved July 26, 2009, from www.nytimes.com.

Burrell, G., & Hearn, J. (1989). The sexuality of organization. In J. Hearn, D. L. Sheppard, P. Tancred-Sheriff, & G. Burrell (Eds.), *The Sexuality of Organization* (pp. 1–28). London: Sage.

Burton, L. J., Barr, C. A., Fink, J. S., & Bruening, J. E. (2009). "Think athletic director, think masculine?": Examination of the gender typing of managerial subroles within athletic administration positions. *Sex Roles, 61*, 416–426.

Calás, M. B., & Smircich, L. (1996). From "the woman's" point of view: Feminist approaches to organization studies. In S. R. Clegg, C. Hardy, & W. R. Nord (eds.), *Handbook of Organization Studies* (pp. 218–257). London: Sage.

Calás, M. B., Smircich, L., & Holvino, E. (2014). Theorizing gender-and-organization: Changing times … changing theories? In S. Kumra, R. Simpson, & R. J. Burke (eds.), *The Oxford Handbook of Gender in Organizations* (pp. 17–52). Oxford: Oxford University Press.

Carli, L. L., & Eagly, A. H. (2016). Women face a labyrinth: An examination of metaphors for women leaders. *Gender in Management: An International Journal, 31*, 514–527.

Carlsen, A., Salam, M., Miller, C. C., Lu, D., Ngu, A., Patel, J. K., & Wichter, Z. (2018, October 29). #MeToo brought down 201 powerful men. Nearly half of their replacements are women. *New York Times.* Retrieved March 16, 2020, from www.nytimes.com.

Carlson, G. (2016, November 12). Gretchen Carlson: My fight against sexual harassment. *New York Times.* Retrieved November 14, 2016, from www.nytimes.com.

Carroll, J. (2006, September 1). Americans prefer male boss to a female boss. *Gallup News Service.* Retrieved May 6, 2009, from http://www.gallup.com.

Carter, N. M., & Silva, C. (2010). Women in management: Delusions of progress. *Harvard Business Review, 88* (3), 19–21.

Choi, N., Fuqua, D. R., & Newman, J. L. (2009). Exploratory and confirmatory studies of the structure of the Bem Sex-Role Inventory short form with two divergent samples. *Educational and Psychological Measurement, 69*, 696–705.

Chrobot-Mason, D., Hoobler, J. M., & Burno, J. (2019). *Lean In* versus the literature: An evidence-based examination. *Academy of Management Perspectives, 33*, 110–130.

Clarke, L. (2007). Sexual harassment law in the United States, the United Kingdom, and the European Union: Discriminatory wrongs and dignitary harms. *Common Law World Review, 36*, 79–105.

Collins, E. G. C., & Blodgett, T. B. (1981). Sexual harassment: Some see it … some won't. *Harvard Business Review, 59* (2), 76–95.

Conger, K., & Wakabayashi, D. (2018, November 8). Google overhauls sexual misconduct policy after employee walkout. *New York Times.* Retrieved November 9, 2018, from www.nytimes.com.

Connell, R. W., & Messerschmidt, J. W. (2005). Hegemonic masculinity: Rethinking the concept. *Gender & Society, 19*, 829–859.

Cook, A., & Glass, C. (2014). Above the glass ceiling: When are women and racial/ethnic minorities promoted to CEO? *Strategic Management Journal, 35*, 1080–1089.

Cortina, L. M., & Berdahl, J. L. (2008). Sexual harassment in organizations: A decade of research in review. In J. Barling & C. L. Cooper, *The Sage Handbook of Organizational Behavior*, Vol. 1 (pp. 469–497). Los Angeles: Sage.

Coston, B. M., & Kimmel, M. (2013). White men as the new victims: Reverse discrimination and the men's rights movement. *Nevada Law Journal, 13*, 368–385.

Creswell, J., Draper, K., & Abrams, R. (2018, April 28). At Nike, revolt led by women leads to exodus of male executives. *New York Times*. Retrieved May 8, 2018, from www.nytimes.com.

Cretella, M. A., Rosik, C. H., & Howsepian, A. A. (2019). Sex and gender are distinct variables critical to health: Comment on Hyde, Bigler, Joel, Tate, and van Anders (2019). *American Psychologist, 74*, 842–844.

Crosby, F. J., Iyer, A., & Sincharoen, S. (2006). Understanding affirmative action. *Annual Review of Psychology, 57*, 585–611.

Davidson, M. J. (1997). *The Black and Ethnic Minority Woman Manager: Cracking the Concrete Ceiling*. London: Chapman.

Davidson, M. J., & Cooper, C. L. (1992). *Shattering the Glass Ceiling: The Woman Manager*. London: Chapman.

Davies, C. M., & Robison, M. (2016). Bridging the gap: An exploration of the use and impact of positive action in the United Kingdom. *International Journal of Discrimination and the Law, 16*, 83–101.

Deaner, R. O., & Smith, B. A. (2012). Sex differences in sports across 50 societies. *Cross-Cultural Research, 47*, 268–309.

Derks, B., Van Laar, C., & Ellemers, N. (2016). The queen bee phenomenon: Why women leaders distance themselves from junior women. *Leadership Quarterly, 27*, 456–469.

Deutsch, F. M. (2007). Undoing gender. *Gender & Society, 21*, 106–127.

Díaz-Sáenz, H. R. (2011). Transformational leadership. In A. Bryman, D. Collinson, K. Grint, B. Jackson, & M. Uhl-Bien (eds.), *The Sage Handbook of Leadership* (pp. 299–310). Los Angeles: Sage.

Dovidio, J. F., Gaertner, S. L., & Kawakam, K. (2010). Racism. In J. F. Dovidio, M. Hewstone, P. Glick, & V. M. Esses (eds.), *The Sage Handbook of Prejudice, Stereotyping, and Discrimination* (pp. 312–327). Los Angeles: Sage.

Draper, K., & Creswell, J. (2018, May 5). Nike's CEO vows changes after claims of workplace harassment and bias. *New York Times*. Retrieved May 8, 2018, from www.nytimes.com.

Eagly, A. H. (1987). *Sex Differences in Social Behavior: A Social-Role Interpretation*. Hillsdale, NJ: Erlbaum.

Eagly, A. H. (1995). The science and politics of comparing women and men. *American Psychologist, 50*, 145–158.

Eagly, A. H. (2018). The shaping of science by ideology: How feminism inspired, led, and constrained scientific understanding of sex and gender. *Journal of Social Issues, 74*, 871–888.

Eagly, A. H., & Carli, L. L. (2003). The female leadership advantage: An evaluation of the evidence. *Leadership Quarterly, 14*, 807–834.

Eagly, A. H., & Chin, J. L. (2010). Diversity and leadership in a changing world. *American Psychologist, 65*, 216–224.

Eagly, A. H., Gartzia, L., & Carli, L. L. (2014). Female advantage: Revisited. In S. Kumra, R. Simpson, & R. J. Burke (eds.), *The Oxford Handbook of Gender in Organizations* (pp. 153–174). Oxford: Oxford University Press.

Eagly, A. H., Johannesen-Schmidt, M. C., & van Engen, M. L. (2003). Transformational, transactional, and laissez-faire leadership styles: A meta-analysis comparing women and men. *Psychological Bulletin, 129*, 569–591.

Eagly, A. H., & Johnson, B. T. (1990). Gender and leadership style: A meta-analysis. *Psychological Bulletin, 108*, 233–256.

Eagly, A. H., & Karau, S. J. (2002). Role congruity theory of prejudice toward female leaders. *Psychological Review, 109*, 573–598.

Eagly, A. H., Karau, S. J., & Makhijani, M. G. (1995). Gender and the effectiveness of leaders: A meta-analysis. *Psychological Bulletin, 117*, 125–145.

Eagly, A. H., Makhijani, M. G., & Klonsky, B. G. (1992). Gender and the evaluation of leaders: A meta-analysis. *Psychological Bulletin, 111*, 3–22.

Eagly, A. H., Nater, C., Miller, D. J., Kaufman, M., & Sczesny, S. (2020). Gender stereotypes have changed: A cross-temporal meta-analysis of U.S. public opinion polls from 1946 to 2018. *American Psychologist, 75*, 301–315.

Eagly, A. H., & Wood, W. (2012). Social role theory. In P. A. M. Van Lange, A. W. Kruglanski, & E. T. Higgins (eds.), *Handbook of Theories of Social Psychology*, Vol. 2 (pp. 458–476). Los Angeles: Sage.

Eagly, A. H., & Wood, W. (2013). The nature-nurture debates: 25 years of challenges in understanding the psychology of gender. *Perspectives on Psychological Science, 8*, 340–357.

Eden, D. (2003). Self-fulfilling prophecies in organizations. In J. Greenberg (ed.), *Organizational Behavior: The State of the Science*, 2nd ed. (pp. 91–122). Mahwah, NJ: Erlbaum.

Ellemers, N. (2018). Gender stereotypes. *Annual Review of Psychology, 69*, 275–298.

Ellemers, N., Rink, F., Derks, B., & Ryan, M. K. (2012). Women in high places: When and why promoting women into top positions can harm them individually or as a group (and how to prevent this). *Research in Organizational Behavior, 32*, 163–187.

Elliott, C., & Stead, V. (2008). Learning from leading women's experience: Towards a sociological understanding. *Leadership, 4*, 159–180.

Ely, R. J., & Padavic, I. (2007). A feminist analysis of organizational research on sex differences. *Academy of Management Review, 32*, 1121–1143.

Ely, R. J., & Padavic, I. (2020). What's really holding women back? It's not what most people think. *Harvard Business Review, 98*(2), 58–67.

Emrich, C. G., Denmark, F. L., & Den Hartog, D. N. (2004). Cross-cultural differences in gender egalitarianism: Implications for societies, organizations, and leaders. In R. J. House, P. J. Hanges, M. Javidan, P. W. Dorfman, & V. Gupta (eds.), *Culture, Leadership, and Organizations: The GLOBE Study of 62 Societies* (pp. 343–394). Thousand Oaks, CA: Sage.

Epstein, C. F. (1973). Positive effects of the multiple negative: Explaining the success of Black professional women. *American Journal of Sociology, 78*, 912–935.

Ezell, H. F., Odewahn, C. A., & Sherman, J. D. (1981). The effects of having been supervised by a woman on perceptions of female managerial competence. *Personnel Psychology, 34*, 291–299.

Ferguson, M., Carlson, D., Boswell, W., Whitten, D., Butts, M. M., & Kacmar, K. M. (2016). Tethered to work: A family systems approach linking mobile device use to turnover intentions. *Journal of Applied Psychology, 101,* 520–534.

Fielden, S. L., & Hunt, C. (2014). Sexual harassment in the workplace. In S. Kumra, R. Simpson, & R. J. Burke (eds.), *The Oxford Handbook of Gender in Organizations* (pp. 353–370). Oxford: Oxford University Press.

Fischhoff, B. (1982). Debiasing. In D. Kahneman, P. Slovic, & A. Tversky (eds.), *Judgment under Uncertainty: Heuristics and Biases* (pp. 422–444). Cambridge: Cambridge University Press.

Fiske, S. T. (1998). Stereotyping, prejudice, and discrimination. In D. T. Gilbert, S. T. Fiske, & G. Lindzey (eds.), *The Handbook of Social Psychology,* Vol. 2 (4th ed., pp. 357–411). Boston: McGraw-Hill.

Fiske, S. T., & Glick, P. (1995). Ambivalence and stereotypes cause sexual harassment: A theory with implications for organizational change. *Journal of Social Issues, 51* (1), 97–115.

Fitzgerald, L. F., Drasgow, F., & Magley, V. J. (1999). Sexual harassment in the armed forces: A test of an integrated model. *Military Psychology, 11,* 329–343.

Foley, S., Kidder, D. L., & Powell, G. N. (2002). The perceived glass ceiling and justice perceptions: An investigation of Hispanic law associates. *Journal of Management, 28,* 471–496.

Fondas, N. (1997). Feminization unveiled: Management qualities in contemporary writing. *Academy of Management Review, 22,* 257–282.

Gardner, W. L., Cogliser, C. C., Davis, K. M., & Dickens, M. P. (2011). Authentic leadership: A review of the literature and research agenda. *Leadership Quarterly, 22,* 1120–1145.

Gatrell, C. J. (2013). Maternal body work: How women managers and professionals negotiate pregnancy and new motherhood at work. *Human Relations, 66,* 621–644.

Gatrell, C., Cooper, C. L., & Kossek, E. E. (eds.). (2010). *Women and Management,* Vols. I and II. Cheltenham: Elgar.

Gatrell, C., Cooper, C. L., & Kossek, E. E. (2017). Maternal bodies as taboo at work: New perspectives on the marginalizing of senior-level women in organizations. *Academy of Management Perspectives, 31,* 239–252.

Gill, R., Kelan, E. K., & Scharff, C. M. (2017). A postfeminist sensibility at work. *Gender, Work and Organization, 24,* 226–244.

Gill, R., & Orgad, S. (2018). The shifting terrain of sex and power: From the "sexualization of culture" to #MeToo. *Sexualities, 21,* 1313–1324.

Glass, C., & Cook, A. (2016). Leading at the top: Understanding women's challenges above the glass ceiling. *Leadership Quarterly, 27,* 51–63.

Glick, P., & Fiske, S. T. (1999). The Ambivalence toward Men Inventory: Differentiating hostile and benevolent beliefs about men. *Psychology of Women Quarterly, 23,* 519–536.

Glick, P., & Rudman, R. A. (2010). Sexism. In J. F. Dovidio, M. Hewstone, P. Glick, & V. M. Esses (eds.), *The Sage Handbook of Prejudice, Stereotyping, and Discrimination* (pp. 328–344). Los Angeles: Sage.

Greenberg, J. (1990). Organizational justice: Yesterday, today, and tomorrow. *Journal of Management, 16,* 399–432.

Greenhaus, J. H., & Powell, G. N. (2017). *Making Work and Family Work: From Hard Choices to Smart Choices.* New York: Routledge

Greer, M. J., & Greene, P. G. (2003). Feminist theory and the study of entrepreneurship. In J. E. Butler (ed.), *New Perspectives on Women Entrepreneurs* (pp. 1–24). Greenwich, CT: Information Age Publishing.

Gruber, J. E., Smith, M., & Kauppinen-Toropainen, K. (1996). Sexual harassment types and severity: Linking research and policy. In M. S. Stockdale (ed.), *Sexual Harassment in the Workplace: Perspectives, Frontiers, and Response Strategies* (pp. 151–173). Thousand Oaks, CA: Sage.

Gupta, V. K., Han, S., Mortal, S. C., Silveri, S. D., & Turban, D. B. (2018). Do women CEOs face greater threat of shareholder activism compared to male CEOs? A role congruity perspective. *Journal of Applied Psychology, 103,* 228–236.

Gupta, V. K., Mortal, S. C., Silveri, S. D., Sun, M., & Turban, D. B. (2020). You're fired! Gender disparities in CEO dismissal. *Journal of Management, 46,* 560–582.

Gutek, B. A. (1985). *Sex and the Workplace: The Impact of Sexual Behavior and Harassment on Women, Men, and Organizations.* San Francisco: Jossey-Bass.

Haines, E. L., Deaux, K., & Lofaro, N. (2016). The times they are a-changing … or are they not? A comparison of gender stereotypes, 1983–2014. *Psychology of Women Quarterly, 40,* 353–363.

Hall, C., & Powell, G. N. (2017, October 20). Men at the top play by different rules. *UConn Today.* Storrs, CT: University of Connecticut. Retrieved October 20, 2017, from https://today.uconn.edu.

Harman, C., & Sealy, R. (2017). Opt-in or opt-out: Exploring how women construe their ambition at early career stages. *Career Development International, 22,* 372–398.

Harrison, D. A., Kravitz, D. A., Mayer, D. M., Leslie, L. M., & Lev-Arey, D. (2006). Understanding attitudes toward affirmative action programs in employment: Summary and meta-analysis of 35 years of research. *Journal of Applied Psychology, 91,* 1013–1036.

Hartmann, H. (1976). Capitalism, patriarchy, and job segregation by sex. *Signs, 1,* 137–169.

Hearn, J., & Parkin, W. (1987). *"Sex" at "Work": The Power and Paradox of Organization Sexuality.* New York: St. Martin's Press.

Heilman, M. E. (1983). Sex bias in work settings: The lack of fit model. In L. L. Cummings & B. M. Staw (eds.), *Research in Organizational Behavior,* Vol. 5 (pp. 269–298). Greenwich, CT: JAI Press.

Heilman, M. E. (2012). Gender stereotypes and workplace bias. *Research in Organizational Behavior, 32,* 113–135.

Hennig, M., & Jardim, A. (1977). *The Managerial Woman.* Garden City, NY: Anchor Press/Doubleday.

Hideg, I., Michela, J. L., & Ferris, D. L. (2011). Overcoming negative reactions of nonbeneficiaries to employment equity: The effect of participation in policy formulation. *Journal of Applied Psychology, 96,* 363–376.

Hilton, J. L., & von Hippel, W. (1996). Stereotypes. *Annual Review of Psychology, 47,* 237–271.

Hofstede, G. (2001). *Culture's Consequences: Comparing Values, Behaviors, Institutions, and Organizations across Nations,* 2nd ed. Thousand Oaks, CA: Sage.

Hoobler, J. M., Lemmon, G., & Wayne, S. J. (2014). Women's managerial aspirations: An organizational development perspective. *Journal of Management, 40,* 703–730.

Horner, M. S. (1972). Toward an understanding of achievement-related conflicts in women. *Journal of Social Issues, 28* (2), 157–175.

Hughes, M. M., Paxton, P., & Krook, M. L. (2017). Gender quotas for legislatures and corporate boards. *Annual Review of Sociology, 43,* 331–352.

Hulin, C. L., Fitzgerald, L. F., & Drasgow, F. (1996). Organizational influences on sexual harassment. In M. S. Stockdale (ed.), *Sexual Harassment in the Workplace: Perspectives, Frontiers, and Response Strategies* (pp. 127–150). Thousand Oaks, CA: Sage.

Hyde, J. S. (2005). The gender similarities hypothesis. *American Psychologist, 60,* 581–592.

Hyde, J. S. (2014). Gender similarities and differences. *Annual Review of Psychology, 65,* 373–398.

Hyde, J. S., Bigler, R. S., Joel, D., Tate, C. C., & van Anders, S. M. (2019). The future of sex and gender in psychology: Five challenges to the gender binary. *American Psychologist, 74,* 171–193.

Hyde, J. S., & Grabe, S. (2008). Meta-analysis in the psychology of women. In F. L. Denmark & M. A. Paludi (eds.), *Psychology of Women: A Handbook of Issues and Theories,* 2nd ed. (pp. 142–173). Westport, CT: Praeger.

Hymowitz, C., & Schellhardt, T. C. (1986, March 24). The glass ceiling: Why women can't seem to break the invisible barrier that blocks them from top jobs. *Wall Street Journal,* pp. 1, 4.

Ilies, R., Hauserman, N., Schwochau, S., & Stibal, J. (2003). Reported incidence rates of work-related sexual harassment in the United States: Using meta-analysis to explain reported rate disparities. *Personnel Psychology, 56,* 607–631.

Jané, S., van Esch, C., & Bilimoria, D. (2018). "Why'd you wanna study that?" A process model of the under-legitimation of a research topic. *Academy of Management Learning and Education, 17,* 401–424.

Jensen, I. W., & Gutek, B. A. (1982). Attributions and assignment of responsibility in sexual harassment. *Journal of Social Issues, 38* (4), 121–136.

Johnson, J. L., Dailey, C. M., & Ellstrand, C. M. (1996). Boards of directors: A review and research agenda. *Journal of Management, 22,* 409–438.

Johnson, S. K., Keplinger, K., Kirk, J. F., & Barnes, L. (2019, July 18). Has sexual harassment at work decreased since #MeToo? *Harvard Business Review.* Retrieved April 21, 2010, from hbr.org.

Jones, T. M. (1991). Ethical decision making by individuals in organizations: An issue-contingent model. *Academy of Management Review, 16,* 366–395.

Joshi, A., Neely, B., Emrich, C., Griffiths, D., & George, G. (2015). Gender research in *AMJ*: An overview of five decades of empirical research and calls to action. *Academy of Management Journal, 58*, 1459–1475.

Judge, T. A., & Piccolo, R. F. (2004). Transformational and transactional leadership: A meta-analytic test of their relative validity. *Journal of Applied Psychology, 89*, 755–768.

Junker, N. M., & van Dick, R. (2014). Implicit theories in organizational settings: A systematic review and research agenda of implicit leadership and followership theories. *Leadership Quarterly, 25*, 1154–1173.

Jurik, N. C., & Siemsen, C. (2009). "Doing gender" as canon or agenda: A symposium on West and Zimmerman. *Gender & Society, 23*, 72–75.

Kanter, R. M. (1977). *Men and Women of the Corporation.* New York: Basic.

Kantor, J., & Twohey, M. (2017, October 5). Harvey Weinstein paid off sexual harassment accusers for decades. *New York Times.* Retrieved December 8, 2017, from www.nytimes.com.

Kantor, J., & Twohey, M. (2019). *She Said: Breaking the Sexual Harassment Story that Helped Ignite a Movement.* New York: Penguin Press.

Kark, R. (2004). The transformational leader: Who is (s)he? A feminist perspective. *Journal of Organizational Change Management, 17*, 160–176.

Kelan, E. K. (2018). Men doing and undoing gender at work: A review and research agenda. *International Journal of Management Reviews, 20*, 544–558.

Kite, M. E., Deaux, K., & Haines, E. L. (2008). Gender stereotypes. In F. L. Denmark & M. A. Paludi (eds.), *Psychology of Women: A Handbook of Issues and Theories,* 2nd ed. (pp. 205–236). Westport, CT: Praeger.

Koch, A. J., D'Mello, S. D., & Sackett, P. R. (2015). A meta-analysis of gender stereotypes and bias in experimental simulations of employment decision making. *Journal of Applied Psychology, 100*, 128–161.

Koenig, A. M., Eagly, A. H., Mitchell, A. A., & Ristikari, T. (2011). Are leader stereotypes masculine? A meta-analysis of three research paradigms. *Psychological Bulletin, 137*, 616–642.

Köllen, T. (2016). Intersexuality and trans-identities within the diversity management discourse. In T. Köllen (ed.), *Sexual Orientation and Transgender Issues in Organizations: Global Perspectives on LGBT Workforce Diversity* (pp. 1–20). Switzerland: Springer.

Komisar, E. (2019, January 16). Masculinity isn't a sickness. *Wall Street Journal.* Retrieved August 16, 2019, from www.wsj.com.

Konrad, A. M., & Linnehan, F. (1999). Affirmative action: History, effects, and attitudes. In G. N. Powell (ed.), *Handbook of Gender and Work* (pp. 429–452). Thousand Oaks, CA: Sage.

Kossek, E. E., Su, R., & Wu, L. (2017). "Opting out" or "pushed out"? Integrating perspectives on women's career equality for gender inclusion and interventions. *Journal of Management, 43*, 228–254.

Kumra, S., Simpson, R., & Burke, R. J. (eds.). (2014). *The Oxford Handbook of Gender in Organizations.* Oxford: Oxford University Press.

Kuperberg, A., & Stone, P. (2008). The media depiction of women who opt out. *Gender & Society, 22*, 497–517.

Larrick, R. P. (2004). Debiasing. In D. J. Koehler & N. Harvey (eds.), *Blackwell Handbook of Judgment and Decision Making* (pp. 316–337). Oxford: Blackwell.

Lenney, E. (1979). Androgyny: Some audacious assertions toward its coming of age. *Sex Roles, 5*, 703–719.

Levine, A., & Crumrine, J. (1975). Women and the fear of success: A problem in replication. *American Journal of Sociology, 80*, 964–974.

Lewis, J. A., Williams, M. G., Peppers, E. J., & Gadson, C. A. (2017). Applying intersectionality to explore the relations between gendered racism and health among Black women. *Journal of Counseling Psychology, 64*, 475–486.

Lewis, P. (2014). Postfeminism, femininities and organization studies: Exploring a new agenda. *Organization Studies, 35*, 1845–1866.

Lippa, R. A. (2005). *Gender, Nature, and Nurture*, 2nd ed. Mahwah, NJ: Erlbaum.

Lorber, J. (1994). *Paradoxes of Gender*. New Haven, CT: Yale University Press.

Lowe, K. B., Kroeck, K. G., & Sivasubramaniam, N. (1996). Effectiveness correlates of transformational and transactional leadership: A meta-analytic review of the MLQ literature. *Leadership Quarterly, 7*, 385–425.

Luthar, H. K., & Luthar, V. K. (2007). A theoretical framework explaining cross-cultural sexual harassment: Integrating Hofstede and Schwartz. *Journal of Labor Research, 28*, 169–188.

Luthar, V. K., & Luthar, H. K. (2002). Using Hofstede's cultural dimensions to explain sexually harassing behaviours in an international context. *International Journal of Human Resource Management, 13*, 268–284.

Lyness, K. S., & Schrader, C. A. (2006). Moving ahead or just moving? An examination of gender differences in senior corporate management appointments. *Group & Organization Management, 31*, 651–676.

Lyonette, C., & Crompton, R. (2015). Sharing the load? Partners' relative earnings and the division of domestic labour. *Work, Employment and Society, 29*, 23–40.

Maccoby, E. E., & Jacklin, C. N. (1974). *The Psychology of Sex Differences*. Stanford, CA: Stanford University Press.

Mack, A. (2003). Inattentional blindness: Looking without seeing. *Current Directions in Psychological Science, 12* (5), 180–184.

MacKinnon, C. A. (1979). *Sexual Harassment of Working Women: A Case of Sex Discrimination*. New Haven, CT: Yale University Press.

Magarey, S. (2018). Beauty becomes political: Beginnings of the Women's Liberation Movement in Australia. *Australian Feminist Studies, 33*, 31–44.

Maier, M. (1999). On the gendered substructure of organization: Dimensions and dilemmas of corporate masculinity. In G. N. Powell (ed.), *Handbook of Gender and Work* (pp. 69–93). Thousand Oaks, CA: Sage.

Mainiero, L. A., & Sullivan, S. E. (2006). *The Opt-out Revolt: Why People Are Leaving Companies to Create Kaleidoscope Careers*. Mountain View, CA: Davies-Black.

Malamuth, N. M., Linz, D., Heavey, C. L., Barnes, G., & Acker, M. (1995). Using the confluence model of sexual aggression to predict men's conflict with women: A 10-year follow-up study. *Journal of Personality and Social Psychology*, *69*, 353–369.

Marshall, J. (1984). *Women Managers: Travellers in a Male World*. Chichester: Wiley.

Martell, R. F., Lane, D. M., & Emrich, C. (1996). Male-female differences: A computer simulation. *American Psychologist*, *51*, 157–158.

Martin, C. L., & Ruble, D. N. (2009). Patterns of gender development. *Annual Review of Psychology*, *61*, 353–381.

Mavin, S. (2006a). Venus envy: Problematizing solidarity behavior and queen bees. *Women in Management Review*, *21*, 264–276.

Mavin, S. (2006b). Venus envy 2: Sisterhood, queen bees, and female misogyny in management. *Women in Management Review*, *21*, pp. 349–364.

Mavin, S., Grandy, G., & Williams, J. (2014). Experiences of women elite leaders doing gender: Intra-gender micro-violence between women. *British Journal of Management*, *25*, 439–455.

McDonald, P. (2012). Workplace sexual harassment 30 years on: A review of the literature. *International Journal of Management Reviews*, *14*, 1–17.

McLaughlin, H., Uggen, C., & Blackstone, A. (2017). The economic and career effects of sexual harassment on working women. *Gender and Society*, *31*, 333–358.

McPherson, M., Smith-Lovin, L., & Cook, J. M. (2001). Birds of a feather: Homophily in social networks. *Annual Review of Sociology*, *27*, 415–444.

Mendes, K., Ringrose, J., & Keller, J. (2018). #MeToo and the promise and pitfalls of challenging rape culture through digital feminist activism. *European Journal of Women's Studies*, *25*, 236–246.

Metz, I., & Kumra, S. (2019). Why are self-help books with career advice for women popular? *Academy of Management Perspectives*, *33*, 82–93.

Miller, D. T. (1999). The norm of self-interest. *American Psychologist*, *54*, 1053–1060.

Milliken, F. J., & Dunn-Jensen, L. M. (2005). The changing time demands of managerial and professional work: Implications for managing the work–life boundary. In E. E. Kossek & S. J. Lambert (eds.), *Work and Life Integration: Organizational, Cultural, and Individual Perspectives* (pp. 43–59). Mahwah, NJ: Erlbaum.

Mintzberg, H., & Van der Hayden, L. (1999). Organigraphs: Drawing how companies really work. *Harvard Business Review*, *77* (5), 87–94.

Morrison, A. M., & Von Glinow, M. A. (1990). Women and minorities in management. *American Psychologist*, *45*, 200–208.

Morrison, A. M., White, R. P., Van Velsor, E., & the Center for Creative Leadership (1987). *Breaking the Glass Ceiling: Can Women Reach the Top of America's Largest Corporations?* Reading, MA: Addison-Wesley.

Morrissey, E. M. (2018). #MeToo spells trouble for them too: Sexual harassment scandals and the corporate board. *Tulane Law Review*, *93*, 177–205.

Motowidlo, S. J. (1986). Information processing in personnel decisions. In K. M. Rowland & G. R. Ferris (eds.), *Research in Personnel and Human Resources Management*, Vol. 4 (pp. 1–44). Greenwich, CT: JAI Press.

Mulcahy, M., & Linehan, C. (2014). Females and precarious board positions: Further evidence of the glass cliff. *British Journal of Management, 25*, 425–438.

Myors, B., Lievens, F., Schollaert, E., Van Hoye, G., Cronshaw, S. F., Mladinic, A., et al. (2008). International perspectives on the legal environment for selection. *Industrial and Organizational Psychology, 1*, 206–246.

Newman, J. (2018, March 16). "Lean in": Five years later. *New York Times*. Retrieved November 1, 2019, from www.nytimes.com.

Nkomo, S. M. (1988). Race and sex: The forgotten case of the black female manager. In S. Rose & L. Larwood (eds.), *Women's Careers: Pathways and Pitfalls* (pp. 133–150). New York: Praeger.

Noon, M. (2010). The shackled runner: Time to rethink positive discrimination? *Work, Employment and Society, 24*, 728–739.

O'Connor, M., Gutek, B. A., Stockdale, M., Geer, T. M., & Melançon, R. (2004). Explaining sexual harassment judgments: Looking beyond gender of the rater. *Law and Human Behavior, 28*, 69–95.

O'Leary-Kelly, A. M., & Bowes-Sperry, L. (2001). Sexual harassment as unethical behavior: The role of moral intensity. *Human Resource Management Review, 11*, 73–92.

O'Leary-Kelly, A. M., Bowes-Sperry, L., Bates, C. A., & Lean, E. R. (2009). Sexual harassment at work: A decade (plus) of progress. *Journal of Management, 35*, 503–536.

O'Leary-Kelly, A. M., Paetzold, R. L., & Griffin, R. W. (2000). Sexual harassment as aggressive behavior: An actor-based perspective. *Academy of Management Review, 25*, 372–388.

Onwuachi-Willig, A. (2018). What about #UsToo? The invisibility of race in the #MeToo movement. *Yale Law Journal Forum, 128*, 105–120.

Padavic, I., Ely, R. J., & Reid, E. M. (2020). Explaining the persistence of gender inequality: The work–family narrative as a social defense against the 24/7 work culture. *Administrative Science Quarterly, 65*, 61–111.

Parker, P. S., & ogilvie, d. t. (1996). Gender, culture, and leadership: Toward a culturally distinct model of African-American women executives' leadership strategies. *Leadership Quarterly, 7*, 189–214.

Parker, T. (2013, January 10). The dawn of the age of female CEOs. *Investopedia*. Retrieved April 15, 2020, from https://finance.yahoo.com.

Parris, D. L., & Peachey, J. W. (2013). A systematic literature review of servant leadership theory in organizational contexts. *Journal of Business Ethics, 113*, 377–393.

Parry, K. W., & Sinha, P. N. (2005). Researching the trainability of transformational leadership. *Human Resource Development International, 8*, 165–183.

Pati, G. C. (1977). Reverse discrimination: What can managers do? *Personnel Journal, 56*, 334–338, 360–362.

Paustian-Underdahl, S. C., Walker, L. S., & Woehr, D. J. (2014). Gender and perceptions of leader effectiveness: A meta-analysis of contextual moderators. *Journal of Applied Psychology, 99*, 1129–1145.

Perlow, L. A. (2012). *Sleeping with Your Smartphone: How to Break the 24/7 Habit and Change the Way You Work.* Boston: Harvard Business Review Press.

Perry, E. L., Davis-Blake, A., & Kulik, C. T. (1994). Explaining gender-based selection decisions: A synthesis of contextual and cognitive approaches. *Academy of Management Review, 19*, 786–820.

Peters, M. A., & Besley, T. (2019). Weinstein, sexual predation, and "Rape Culture": Public pedagogies and Hashtag Internet activism. *Educational Philosophy and Theory, 51*, 458–464.

Petter, O. (2018, November 20). Toxic masculinity leaves most young men feeling pressured to "man up." *Independent.* Retrieved August 16, 2019, from www.independent.co.uk.

Pew Research Center. (2015, January 14). *Women CEOs in Fortune 500 companies, 1995–2018.* Washington, DC: Pew Research Center. Retrieved April 13, 2020, from www.pewsocialtrends.org.

Piazza, J. (2016, September 27). Women of color hit a "concrete ceiling" in business. *Wall Street Journal.* Retrieved July 3, 2017, from www.wsj.com.

Powell, G. N. (1988). *Women and Men in Management.* Newbury Park, CA: Sage.

Powell, G. N. (1993). *Women and Men in Management,* 2nd ed. Newbury Park, CA: Sage.

Powell, G. N. (1998). The abusive organization. *Academy of Management Executive, 12* (2), 95–96.

Powell, G. N. (1999). Reflections on the glass ceiling: Recent trends and future prospects. In G. N. Powell (ed.), *Handbook of Gender and Work* (pp. 325–345). Thousand Oaks, CA: Sage.

Powell, G. N. (2009, August 2). A transformational style. *New York Times.* Retrieved August 2, 2009, from http://roomfordebate.blogs.nytimes.com.

Powell, G. N. (2011). *Women and Men in Management,* 4th ed. Los Angeles: Sage.

Powell, G. N. (2019). *Women and Men in Management,* 5th ed. Los Angeles: Sage.

Powell, G. N., & Butterfield, D. A. (1979). The "good manager": Masculine or androgynous? *Academy of Management Journal, 22*, 395–403.

Powell, G. N., & Butterfield, D. A. (1989). The "good manager": Did androgyny fare better in the 1980s? *Group & Organization Studies, 14*, 216–233.

Powell, G. N., & Butterfield, D. A. (1994). Investigating the "glass ceiling" phenomenon: An empirical study of actual promotions to top management. *Academy of Management Journal, 37*, 68–86.

Powell, G. N., & Butterfield, D. A. (1997). Effect of race on promotions to top management in a federal department. *Academy of Management Journal, 40*, 112–128.

Powell, G. N., & Butterfield, D. A. (2011). Sex, gender, & the U.S. presidency: Ready for a female president? *Gender in Management: An International Journal, 26*, 394–40.

Powell, G. N., & Butterfield, D. A. (2013). Sex, gender, and aspirations to top management: Who's opting out? Who's opting in? *Journal of Vocational Behavior*, *82*, 30–36.

Powell, G. N., & Butterfield, D. A. (2015a). Correspondence between self- and good-manager descriptions: Examining stability and change over four decades. *Journal of Management*, *41*, 1745–1773.

Powell, G. N., & Butterfield, D. A. (2015b). The glass ceiling: What have we learned 20 years on? *Journal of Organizational Effectiveness: People and Performance*, *2*, 306–326.

Powell, G. N., & Butterfield, D. A. (2015c). The preference to work for a man or a woman: A matter of sex and gender? *Journal of Vocational Behavior*, *86*, 28–37.

Powell, G. N., Butterfield, D. A., & Bartol, K. M. (2008). Leader evaluations: A new female advantage? *Gender in Management: An International Journal*, *23*, 156–174.

Powell, G. N., Butterfield, D. A., & Jiang, X. (2018). Why Trump and Clinton won and lost: The roles of hypermasculinity and androgyny. *Equality, Diversity, and Inclusion: An International Journal*, *37*, 44–62.

Powell, G. N., Butterfield, D. A., & Parent, J. D. (2002). Gender and managerial stereotypes: Have the times changed? *Journal of Management*, *28*, 177–193.

Powell, G. N., & Graves, L. M. (2003). *Women and Men in Management*, 3rd ed. Thousand Oaks, CA: Sage.

Pryor, J. B., Giedd, J. L., & Williams, K. B. (1995). A social psychological model for predicting sexual harassment. *Journal of Social Issues*, *51* (1), 69–84.

Ransom, J. (2020, February 24). Harvey Weinstein is found guilty of sex crimes in #MeToo watershed. *New York Times*. Retrieved February 24, 2020, from www.nytimes.com.

Raven, B. H. (1993). The bases of power: Origins and recent developments. *Journal of Social Issues*, *49* (4), 227–251.

Raver, J. A., & Gelfand, M. J. (2005). Beyond the individual victim: Linking sexual harassment, team processes, and team performance. *Academy of Management Journal*, *48*, 387–400.

Redden, M. (2016, July 21). Roger Ailes accused of harassment by at least 20 women, attorneys say. *The Guardian*. Retrieved March 30, 2020, from www.theguardian.com.

Reid, P. T. (1988). Racism and sexism: Comparisons and conflicts. In P. A. Katz & D. A. Taylor (eds.), *Eliminating Racism: Profiles in Controversy* (pp. 203–221). New York: Plenum.

Reilly, D. (2019). Gender can be a continuous variable, not just a categorical one: Comment on Hyde, Bigler, Joel, Tate, and van Anders (2019). *American Psychologist*, *74*, 840–841.

Reuben, E., Rey-Biel, P., Sapienza, P., & Zingales, L. (2012). The emergence of male leadership in competitive environments. *Journal of Economic Behavior and Organization*, *83*, 111–117.

Ridgeway, C. L. (1991). The social construction of status value: Gender and other nominal characteristics. *Social Forces, 70*, 367–386.

Ridgeway, C. L. (2006). Gender as an organizing force in social relations: Implications for the future of inequality. In F. D. Blau, M. C. Brinton, & D. B. Grusky (eds.). *The Declining Significance of Gender?* (pp. 265–287). New York: Russell Sage Foundation.

Ridgeway, C. L., & Kricheli-Katz, T. (2013). Intersecting cultural beliefs in social relations: Gender, race, and class binds and freedoms. *Gender & Society, 27*, 294–318.

Riger, S., & Galligan, P. (1980). Women in management: An exploration of competing paradigms. *American Psychologist, 35*, 902–910.

Risman, B. J. (2004). Gender as a social structure: Theory wrestling with activism. *Gender & Society, 18*, 429–450.

Risman, B. J. (2009). From doing to undoing: Gender as we know it. *Gender & Society, 23*, 81–84.

Rodriguez, J. K., Holvino, E., Fletcher, J. K., & Nkomo, S. M. (2016). The theory and praxis of intersectionality in work and organisations: Where do we go from here? *Gender, Work and Organization, 23*, 201–222.

Roehling, M. V., & Huang, J. (2018). Sexual harassment training effectiveness: An interdisciplinary review and call for research. *Journal of Organizational Behavior, 39*, 134–150.

Room for debate: Do women make better bosses? (2009, August 2). *New York Times*. Retrieved August 2, 2009, from http://roomfordebate.blogs.nytimes.com.

Rosette, A. S., de Leon, R. P., Koval, C. Z., & Harrison, D. A. (2018). Intersectionality: Connecting experiences of gender with race at work. *Research in Organizational Behavior, 38*, 1–22.

Rosette, A. S., Koval, C. Z., Ma, A., & Livingston, R. (2016). Race matters for women leaders: Intersectional effects on agentic deficiencies and penalties. *Leadership Quarterly, 27*, 429–445.

Rosette, A. S., & Livingston, R. W. (2012). Failure is not an option for Black women: Effects of organizational performance on leaders with single versus dual-subordinate identities. *Journal of Experimental Social Psychology, 48*, 1162–1167.

Ross, S. M., & Offermann, L. R. (1997). Transformational leaders: Measurement of personality attributes and work group performance. *Personality and Social Psychology Bulletin, 23*, 1078–1086.

Rothbart, M. (1981). Memory processes and social beliefs. In D. L. Hamilton (ed.), *Cognitive Processes in Stereotyping and Intergroup Behavior* (pp. 145–181). Hillsdale, NJ: Erlbaum.

Rotundo, M., Nguyen, D.-H., & Sackett, P. R. (2001). A meta-analytic review of gender differences in perceptions of sexual harassment. *Journal of Applied Psychology, 86*, 914–922.

Rudman, L. A., & Glick, P. (2001). Prescriptive gender stereotypes and backlash toward agentic women. *Journal of Social Issues, 57*, 743–762.

Ryan, M. K., & Haslam, S. A. (2005). The glass cliff: Evidence that women are over-represented in precarious leadership positions. *British Journal of Management, 16,* 81–90.

Ryan, M. K., Haslam, S. A., Hersby, M. D., & Bongiorno, R. (2011). Think crisis – think female: The glass cliff and contextual variation in the think manager – think male stereotype. *Journal of Applied Psychology, 96,* 470–484.

Ryan, M. K., Haslam, S. A., Morgenroth, T., Rink, F., Stoker, J., & Peters, K. (2016). Getting on top of the glass cliff: Reviewing a decade of evidence, explanations, and impact. *Leadership Quarterly, 27,* 446–455.

Saguy, A. C. (2018). Europeanization or national specificity? Legal approaches to sexual harassment in France, 2002–2012. *Law & Society Review, 52,* 140–171.

Sanchez-Hucles, J. V., & Davis, D. D. (2010). Women and women of color in leadership: Complexity, identity, and intersectionality. *American Psychologist, 65,* 171–181.

Sandberg, S. (2013). *Lean In: Women, Work, and the Will to Lead.* New York: Knopf.

Schein, V. E. (1973). The relationship between sex role stereotypes and requisite management characteristics. *Journal of Applied Psychology, 57,* 95–100.

Schein, V. E. (1975). Relationships between sex role stereotypes and requisite management characteristics among female managers. *Journal of Applied Psychology, 60,* 340–344.

Schein, V. E., Mueller, R., Lituchy, T., & Liu, J. (1996). Think manager – think male: A global phenomenon? *Journal of Organizational Behavior, 17,* 33–41.

Sedmak, N. J., & Vidas, C. (1994). *Primer of Equal Employment Opportunity,* 6th ed. Washington, DC: Bureau of National Affairs.

Seron, C., Silbey, S. S., Cech, E., & Rubineau, B. (2016). Persistence is cultural: Professional socialization and the reproduction of sex segregation. *Work and Occupations, 43,* 178–214.

Sharpe, R. (2000, November 20). As leaders, women rule. *Business Week,* 74–84.

Shin, Y. (2012). CEO ethical leadership, ethical climate, climate strength, and collective organizational citizenship behavior. *Journal of Business Ethics, 108,* 299–312.

Simmons, W. W. (2001, January 11). When it comes to choosing a boss, Americans still prefer men. *Gallup News Service.* Retrieved September 10, 2001, from www.gallup.com.

Simons, D. J., & Rensink, R. A. (2005). Change blindness: Past, present, and future. *Trends in Cognitive Sciences, 9,* 16–20.

Sleek, S. (2015). How brains think. *Observer: Association for Psychological Science,* 28 (5), 21.

Smith, A. N., Watkins, M. B., Ladge, J. J., & Carlton, P. (2019). Making the invisible visible: Paradoxical effects of intersectional invisibility on the career experiences of executive Black women in the workplace. *Academy of Management Journal, 62:* 1705–1734.

Smith, P., Caputi, P., & Crittenden, N. (2012). A maze of metaphors around glass ceilings. *Gender in Management: An International Journal, 27,* 436–448.

Smooth, W. G. (2010). Intersectionalities of race and gender and leadership. In K. O'Connor (ed.), *Gender and Women's Leadership: A Reference Handbook*, Vol. 1 (pp. 31–40). Los Angeles: Sage.

Staines, G., Tavris, C., & Jayaratne, T. E. (1973). The queen bee syndrome. *Psychology Today, 7* (8), 55–60.

Steel, E., & Schmidt, M. S. (2017, April 1). Bill O'Reilly thrives at Fox News, even as harassment settlements pile up. *New York Times*. Retrieved March 30, 2020, from www.nytimes.com.

Stempel, J. (2017, November 20). 21st Century Fox in $90 million settlement tied to sexual harassment scandal. *Reuters*. Retrieved March 30, 2020, from www.reuters.com.

Stogdill, R. M. (1974). *Handbook of Leadership*. New York: Free Press.

Stumpf, S. A., & London, M. (1981). Management promotions: Individual and organizational factors influencing the decision process. *Academy of Management Review, 6*, 539–549.

Tajfel, H., & Turner, J. C. (1986). The social identity theory of intergroup behavior. In S. Worchel & W. G. Austin (eds.), *Psychology of Intergroup Relations*, 2nd ed. (pp. 7–24). Chicago: Nelson-Hall.

Tangri, S. S., Burt, M. R., & Johnson, L. B. (1982). Sexual harassment at work: Three explanatory models. *Journal of Social Issues, 38* (4), 33–54.

Tenbrunsel, A. E., Rees, M. R., & Diekmann, K. A. (2019). Sexual harassment in academia: Ethical climates and bounded ethicality. *Annual Review of Psychology, 70*, 245–270.

Thacker, R. A., & Ferris, G. R. (1991). Understanding sexual harassment in the workplace: The influence of power and politics within the dyadic interaction of harasser and target. *Human Resource Management Review, 1*, 23–37.

Uggen, C., & Blackstone, A. (2004). Sexual harassment as a gendered expression of power. *American Sociological Review, 69*, 64–92.

UK Government. (2010). *Equality Act 2010: Section 26, Harassment*. Retrieved February 14, 2020, from www.legislation.gov.uk.

Unger, R. K. (1979). Toward a redefinition of sex and gender. *American Psychologist, 34*, 1085–1094.

US Department of Labor. (1991). *A Report on the Glass Ceiling Initiative*. Washington, DC: US Department of Labor.

US Equal Employment Opportunity Commission. (2016). Code of Federal Regulations, Title 29 – Labor, Part 1604 – Guidelines on discrimination because of sex, Section 1604.11 – Sexual harassment. Retrieved December 1, 2017, from www.gpo.gov.

US Merit Systems Protection Board. (1995). *Sexual Harassment in the Federal Workplace: Trends, Progress, and Continuing Challenges*. Washington, DC: Government Printing Office.

US Merit Systems Protection Board. (2018). *Research Brief: Update on Sexual Harassment in the Federal Workplace*. Washington, DC: US Merit Systems Protection Board. Retrieved February 21, 2020, from www.mspb.gov.

Vecchio, R. P. (2002). Leadership and gender advantage. *Leadership Quarterly, 13,* 643–671.

Vial, A. C., Napier, J. L., & Brescoll, V. L. (2016). A bed of thorns: Female leaders and the self-reinforcing cycle of illegitimacy. *Leadership Quarterly, 27,* 400–414.

Vinnicombe, S., Burke, R. J., Blake-Beard, S., & Moore, L. L. (eds.). (2013). *Handbook of Research on Promoting Women's Careers.* Cheltenham: Elgar.

Wakabayashi, D., & Benner, K. (2018, October 25). How Google protected Andy Rubin, the "father of Android." *New York Times.* Retrieved November 9, 2018, from www.nytimes.com.

Wang, G., Oh, I.-S., Courtright, S. H., & Colbert, A. E. (2011). Transformational leadership and performance across criteria and levels: A meta-analytic review of 25 years of research. *Group & Organization Management, 36,* 223–270.

Wang, M., & Kelan, E. (2013). The gender quota and female leadership: Effects of the Norwegian gender quota on board chairs and CEOs. *Journal of Business Ethics, 117,* 449–466.

Warren, T. (2011). Researching the gender division of unpaid domestic work: Practices, relationships, negotiations, and meanings. *Sociological Review, 59,* 129–148.

Way, N. (2019). Reimagining boys in the 21st century. *Men and Masculinities, 22,* 926–929.

West, C., & Fenstermaker, S. (1995). Doing difference. *Gender & Society, 9,* 8–37.

West, C., & Zimmerman, D. H. (1987). Doing gender. *Gender & Society, 1,* 125–151.

West, C., & Zimmerman, D. H. (2009). Accounting for doing gender. *Gender & Society, 23,* 112–122.

Whippman, R. (2019, October 10). Enough leaning in. Let's tell men to lean out. *New York Times.* Retrieved October 17, 2019, from www.nytimes.com.

Williams, J. C., Blair-Loy, M., & Berdahl, J. L. (2013). Cultural schemas, social class, and the flexibility stigma. *Journal of Social Issues, 69,* 209–234.

Willness, C. R., Steel, P., & Lee, K. (2007). A meta-analysis of the antecedents and consequences of workplace sexual harassment. *Personnel Psychology, 60,* 127–162.

Wood, W., & Eagly, A. H. (2010). Gender. In S. T. Fiske, D. T. Gilbert, & G. Lindzey (eds.), *Handbook of Social Psychology,* 5th ed., Vol. 1 (pp. 629–667). New York: Wiley.

Woolley, H. T. (1910). A review of the recent literature on the psychology of sex. *Psychological Bulletin, 7,* 335–342.

XpertHR. (2020). What is the difference between positive action and positive discrimination? *XpertHR.* Retrieved January 22, 2020, from www.xperthr.co.uk.

Yelton-Stanley, S. K., & Howard, A. M. (2000). Women's liberation movement. In A. M. Howard & F. M. Kavenik (eds.), *Handbook of American Women's History* (pp. 640–641). Thousand Oaks, CA: Sage.

Zarya, V. (2018, May 21). The share of female CEOs in the Fortune 500 dropped by 25% in 2018. *Fortune*. Retrieved June 26, 2019, from https://fortune.com.

Zillman, C. (2019, May 16). The Fortune 500 has more female CEOs than ever before. *Fortune*. Retrieved September 17, 2019, from https://fortune.com.

Zippel, K. (2009). The European Union 2002 directive on sexual harassment: A feminist success? *Comparative European Politics, 7,* 139–157.

INDEX

abusive organizational cultures 25, 82
Ailes, Roger 84
American Psychological Association 2, 11
androgyny 11–13
Australia: EEO legislation 50

Bem Sex-Role Inventory 12, 13, 17, 43, 64
biases:
  against women as bosses 42, 44
  and debiasing 78–80
  in decision-makers' evaluations of
    women 25, 27, 30
  and gender differences/similarities 5–6
  see also discrimination; stereotyping
boards of directors:
  and appointment of CEOs 79
  and sexual harassment 73–4, 84–5
books by women in top management 25–6
Brady, Karen 25
Burke, Tarana 75
Butterfield, Tony
  research with Gary Powell 6–7, 12–13,
    25, 43
  glass ceiling 33–7, 81

Canada: EEO legislation 50
change blindness 78
charisma in leadership 46–7, 48
chief executive officers (CEOs):
  and boards of directors 73, 84, 85
  and sexual harassment 84, 85
  women as 2, 21–2, 29, 74, 75, 79, 85
  see also decision-making for
    promotions; women as bosses
class 32
Clinton, Hillary 13
contingent rewards 47
criteria for promotions 34

debiasing 78–80
decision-making for promotions 21–38,
    78–9
  criteria for promotions 34
  decision-makers' schemas (mental
    models) 27
  fear of success 23, 24
  feminist theories 30, 31
    Marxist theories 32
  gender-based jobholder schemas 79
  glass ceiling 22–3
  glass ceilings, research by Powell and
    Butterfield 33–7, 81
  human capital 34, 35, 76, 81
  line/staff functions 28
  minimizing uncertainty 27–8
  person-centered theories 23–6
  promotion records 81
  proportion of women in management
    6, 7, 9, 12, 13, 17, 22
  CEOs 2, 21–2, 25
  SES procedure 34–6, 81
  situation-centered theories 26–30
  social-system-centered theories 30–33
  "think manager – think male"
    paradigm 14, 17, 27, 29
  training in decision-making 79–80
  women's fluctuating hormones 28
  see also female advantage/
    disadvantage; glass ceiling; women
    as bosses
Denmark: EEO legislation 50
discrimination:
  and evaluations of human capital 34
  glass cliffs 29
  human capital 34
  intentionality 29–30
  minimizing 37

and "positive discrimination" 37, 51, 52
"positive/reverse discrimination" 51, 52
racial/ethnic 64
and sexual harassment 69
and stereotyping 10
and women's liberation movement 6
see also equal employment opportunity
    (EEO) laws;gender stereotypes
distributive justice 23
doing gender 30–31, 76, 77

Eagly, Alice 44
educational attainment and promotions
    27
equal employment opportunity (EEO)
    laws 36, 50–52, 55, 83
    legal mandates 51–2
    positive action 50–51
European Union:
    definitions of sexual harassment 60
    Employment Equality Framework
        Directive 50

fear of success 23, 24
female advantage/disadvantage 39–41, 55
    in leadership styles 48–50
    women of color 52–4
feminist theories 30, 31
    Marxist theories 32
Financial Times Stock Exchange (FTSE)
    100 companies 21
flexible working hours 82
Fortune 500 companies 21–2
Fox News 84

Gallup Organization 41
"gender": definitions 3–4
gender differences/similarities:
    and gender stereotypes 5
    and leadership style 47–8, 74
    measurements of 5–6
gender egalitarianism 69, 72
    see also equal employment opportunity
        (EEO) laws
gender fatigue 1–2
gender roles:
    definition 3
    and leadership roles 48

gender and sex 3–4
gender and sexuality 67–8
gender as social structure 31
gender stereotypes:
    and androgyny 11–13
    in children's books 6
    and gender differences/similarities 5
    and leadership styles 47–9
    linkage with leader stereotypes 11–17
    in middle management 49
    see also leader stereotypes
gender-class-race intersection 32
gendered jobs advertising 6
gendering social systems 31, 76–7
glass ceiling 22–3, 33–7, 81
glass cliffs 28–9
glass walls 28
GLOBE study 69
"good managers" and androgynous 12, 13
Google 58
Graves, Laura 44

hierarchies 15
    and class 32
    and male dominance (patriarchy) 30,
        32, 67, 68
    and power differentials 65, 67
    and sexual harassment 61, 67, 71
homosocial reproduction 27
hub structure 15
human capital 34, 35, 76, 81

"ideal presidents", traits of 13
individualism 43, 68, 72
individualized consideration in leadership
    47
inspirational motivation in leadership 47
intellectual stimulation in leadership 47
intersectional invisibility 54
intersectionality 4–5
intersex people 4

Japan: EEO legislation 50

lack of fit model 16, 27
laissez-faire leadership 47–8, 80
leader effectiveness 40, 46, 48, 49–50,
    80, 81

leader preferences polls 41–3
  age and gender of respondents 42
  age of respondents 42
  gender identity of respondents 43
  gender of respondents and current
    boss 42
leader stereotypes:
  effects on behavior 20
  linkage with gender stereotypes 11–17
  in promotions 27
  race and ethnicity 20
  social-system-centered theories 14–15
  and traits of "good managers" 12, 13
  traits of "ideal presidents" 13
  see also gender stereotypes
leadership styles 46–50
  female advantage 48–9, 50
  and female gender roles 48
  and gender differences 47–8, 80
  "hyper-masculine" style 2
  laissez-faire 47–8
  male advantage 49–50
  meta-analyses 48–9, 49–50
  and perceptions of effectiveness 49–50
  styles by name 46
  transactional 46, 47, 48
  transformational 19, 46–7, 48
  women of color 54
leadership training 73, 80–81
Lean In Circles 26
line/staff functions 28

management by exception 47
masculinity and femininity 10–11
  and androgyny 11–13, 17
  and aspiration to top management 25
  and management traits: change over
    time 16–17
  masculinity-femininity dimensions 64,
    69, 72
  in occupations 13–14
  and role congruity 15
  and traits for success 23–4
  see also female advantage/
    disadvantage; gender stereotyping
#Me Too movement 2, 57, 58, 69, 74–5, 84
  possible negative effects 75
middle managers 14, 28, 49, 61
Milano, Alyssa 75

national cultures 68, 72
nature and nurture 77–8
Netherlands: EEO legislation 50
New York Times 44
Nike 58
Norway 73

opting out 24, 25, 82
O'Reilly, Billy 84
organizations:
  demands for long working hours 82
  effectiveness 22, 23, 37
  equal opportunities 51, 83
  expectations/pressure on managers
    25, 82
  flexible work 82
  gender composition and sexual
    harassment 66
  gender and sexuality 67–8
  gendered structures 31
  hierarchies and power differentials 65, 67
  hierarchy and power differentials 65
    and sexual harassment 65, 67, 71
  sexual harassment 73–4, 83–4
    boards of directors 73–4, 84–5
    stockholders 84
    training programs 73

patriarchy 14, 30, 32
  and sexuality 67–8
performance evaluation 22, 47
  computer simulaion 5–6
  women of color 29, 53
person-centered theories 4, 77
  decision-making for promotions 16,
    23–6
  female advantage/disadvantage 40
  sexual harassment 62–5, 70
postfeminist sensibility 2
Powell, G.N. 82
  debate on women as bosses 44–6
  research with Tony Butterfield 6–7,
    12–13, 16–17, 33–7, 43
  Women and Men in Management 7, 9, 76
power 65, 67, 68, 72
precariousness of top positions (glass cliff)
  28–9
prejudice 10, 40, 52, 53
  see also discrimination

procedural and distributive justice in decision-making 22–3
proportion of women in management 6, 7, 9, 12, 13, 17, 22
CEOs 2, 21–2, 75

race and ethnicity 4–5, 20, 29, 32
  prejudice 40, 53
  see also women of color
research interest in gender-leadership linkage 1–2
role congruity theory 15, 27

Sandberg, Sheryl 25
  Lean In: Women, Work and the Will to Lead 26
sex and gender 3–4
sexual harassment 2, 8, 57–75
  actions against harassment 73, 75
  as aggression 64
  corporate action 58
  definitions 59–60, 61–2, 79
    gender differences 61
  effects of 62–3
  as ethical/moral choice 63, 70–71
  hostile environment sexual harassment 70
  #Me Too movement 2, 57, 58, 69, 74–5, 84
  person-centered theories 62–5, 70
    individual differences model 63–4
    natural/biological model 62–3
  quid pro quo harassment 70
  situation-centered theories 65–7, 71
    ethical cultures 66
    gender composition of work environment 66
    organizational hierarchy and power 65, 71
    presence of observers 66–7
  social-system-centered theories 67–9, 71–2
    gender and sexuality 67–8, 72
    masculinity-femininity dimension 69
    national cultures 68
    national power distances 68, 72
    patriarchal societies 67
  targets 62, 64
  tolerance 72

training programs 73
types of sexual oriented behaviors 61
Weinstein allegations 57–8, 59, 69–74, 84
  behaviors 70
  women of color 64, 75
situation-centered theories 4, 77
  decision-making for promotions 26–30
  female advantage/disadvantage 40–41
  sexual harassment 65–7, 71
Smith, Carol 44
social-system-centered theories 4, 76, 77
  decision-making for promotions 30–33
  leader stereotypes 14–15
  sexual harassment 67–9, 71–2
status characteristics theory 15
stereotyping 9–20, 78
  change over time 16–19
  cognitive and social processes 17–18
  definition 9
  gender and leader stereotypes 6, 7, 10–14, 78
  and practice of management 20
  and prejudice 10, 40
  theories 14–16, 17–19
Stogdill, R.M.
  Handbook of Leadership (1974) 11
success and masculinity/femininity 23

terminology 3–4
theories of gender-leadership linkage 4–6
"think manager – think male" paradigm 14, 17, 27, 29
training in decision-making 79–80
transactional leadership 46, 47, 48
transformational leadership 19, 46–7, 48
  and female leaders 48
transgender people 4
Trump, Donald 2, 13

uncertainty in decision-making 27–8
undoing gender 8, 76, 77
United Kingdom:
  definitions of sexual harassment 59
  EEO legislation 50–51
USA:
  definitions of sexual harassment 59–60
  equal employment opportunities (EEO) legislation 36, 50, 51–2

gender egalitarianism 72
individualism 72
power distance 72
Senior Executive Service (SES):
    employment procedures 33–7, 81

web structure 15
Weinstein, Harvey 57–8, 59, 69–74, 84
women as bosses 43–50, 79
    online debate 44–6
women of color 29, 52–4, 55–6
    advantage 41, 52–3

concrete ceiling 22, 32–3
"double whammy" 53
intersectional invisibility 54
and leadership styles 54
prejudice 40, 53
sexual harassment 64, 75
women hindered by other women 29
women as weaker gender 63
women's fluctuating hormones 28
women's liberation movement 6
women's studies (gender studies) 6
working hours 82

Lightning Source UK Ltd.
Milton Keynes UK
UKHW022212050521
383159UK00004B/260